Money

THE ART OF LIVING SERIES
Series Editor: Mark Vernon

From Plato to Bertrand Russell philosophers have engaged wide audiences on matters of life and death. *The Art of Living* series aims to open up philosophy's riches to a wider public once again. Taking its lead from the concerns of the ancient Greek philosophers, the series asks the question "How should we live?". Authors draw on their own personal reflections to write philosophy that seeks to enrich, stimulate and challenge the reader's thoughts about their own life.

Published
Clothes *John Harvey*
Death *Todd May*
Deception *Ziyad Marar*
Faith *Theo Hobson*
Fame *Mark Rowlands*
Hunger *Raymond Tallis*
Illness *Havi Carel*
Me *Mel Thompson*
Middle Age *Christopher Hamilton*
Money *Eric Lonergan*
Pets *Erica Fudge*
Sport *Colin McGinn*
Wellbeing *Mark Vernon*
Work *Lars Svendsen*

Forthcoming
Commitment *Piers Benn*
Empathy *Roman Krznaric*
Forgiveness *Eve Garrad & David McNaughton*
Self-Love *John Lippitt*
Sex *Seiriol Morgan*
Science *Steve Fuller*

Money

Eric Lonergan

ACUMEN

320185536

2-2-10

© Eric Lonergan, 2009

First published in 2009 by Acumen

Acumen Publishing Limited
4 Saddler Street
Durham
DH1 3NP
www.acumenpublishing.co.uk

ISBN: 978-1-84465-203-7

British Library Cataloguing-in-Publication Data
A catalogue record for this book is available
from the British Library.

Typeset in Warnock Pro.
Printed in the UK by the MPG Books Group.

Contents

Acknowledgements

This book would not have happened without Roman Krznaric – a great friend and inspiration. It also would not have happened without Mark Vernon and Steven Gerrard. Thanks, Mark, for the discussions, ideas and encouragement. I also owe a great debt to Steven Gerrard at Acumen for the opportunity to write this book, and for his suggestions and thoughts. Thanks also to Kate Williams for excellent copy-editing and comments. Dave Fishwick, at M&G, has not just been great to "work" with, but also has had a profound influence on my thinking. Many friends and colleagues have read drafts and given feedback. Thanks to Paddy Boyle, Philip Coggan, Tony Finding, Tristan Hanson, Joseph Little, Daniel Mytnik, Juan Nevado, Jenny Rodgers, Craig Simpson, Rupert Taylor and Sean Wade. Discussions with Richard and Leslie Ely have helped in many ways, and so has their support. I am also grateful to Patrizio Salvadori, for giving me a copy of Bertrand Russell's *Problems of Philosophy* many years ago, and Martin Bates, for giving me my first copy of Adam Smith's *Wealth of Nations* more recently. To Corinna Salvadori Lonergan: *grazie di cuore*.

My deepest gratitude is to my wife, Jo, for all her help, and to Gina and Maia for theirs.

Eric Lonergan

Introduction

I remember the first one pound note I owned. I must have been eight or nine years old. We lived on a cul-de-sac in Dublin, and my friends and I would loiter at various corners of the road. A friend's older brother was with us that day, and when he was around he assumed leadership. We instinctively competed for his patronage. I remember pulling the note out from my pocket, carefully and surreptitiously, so that one third of it was showing. Finally, it caught his eye: "Hey! Lonergan's got a pound". I was teased for the obviousness of my bid for attention, but only briefly: I had risen in his regard. After all, I had a pound.

Twenty years later I work for an investment bank in London. It is a world centred on money. We trade and advise clients for profit. Many colleagues obsess about how much they are paid, and how this compares to their peers. I care about how much I earn too, but mostly I enjoy my work. I am fascinated by why currency, bond and stock prices fluctuate. It is exciting and cerebral. Interaction is less personal the greater the number of participants. Markets connect a great many, so they are abstract and quantitative. But always human. Mood and perspective can swiftly change.

On rare occasions what I do gives me a glimpse into a dark future. And then I feel futile. Markets foresee problems, like an alarm that rings before the fire has started. I can see what's happening, and can do nothing about it. That is how I felt during the Asian crisis. It started as an intellectual problem: an arcane debate in international economics on the relative merits of fixed or floating exchange rates.

A series of runs on the Thai exchange rate eventually precipitated its collapse in July 1997. Watching the predictable panic spread from one Asian country to another was like witnessing the future in slow motion. The recession that followed had extreme social and human consequences. In one of the poorest and most populous countries in the region, Indonesia, it led to the killing of perhaps thousands of ethnic Chinese in the cities of Jakarta and Solo, and shortly afterwards the overthrow of the Suharto dictatorship. I witnessed this at some distance. Periodically I travelled to the region to meet with policy-makers and colleagues, but I did not live there.

On 10 October 2008, these memories of the Asian crisis returned. This time the crisis and panic were unfolding closer to home, as fear of financial failure spread throughout the entire Western banking system. On that day, there was a genuine risk that the system of money that ties the developed world together would break down. The payment mechanism that mediates most forms of social interaction was at risk of collapse.

How does this happen: how do money, banking and the prices of financial instruments have the potential to threaten social stability? In this book I shall attempt to answer this question. In doing so, I shall also reveal much more about money. Despite its central role in our lives and societies, money is very poorly understood. Many of our attitudes and beliefs about debt, savings and financial markets are little better than prejudices, or confused value judgements that have somehow survived for hundreds of years. Economics dispels some of this confusion, but has separate flaws. It ignores many of the most important properties of money: how money and prices affect our beliefs, values and feelings. In economics, money is an instrument that serves our objectives and never independently affects us.

This is why convincing explanations of recessions and panics are absent from economic textbooks. In the main, economics assumes that people form beliefs based on an objective assessment of the facts: that we are not affected by the process of exchange itself or social interaction. My experience of human psychology is very different. I view reason as a capacity we possess with the potential for enlightenment, but which we often ignore and struggle to apply. When our capacity to reason is limited by either ability or circumstance, we are still able to act. We resort to rules of thumb, which may work on average or in very different circumstances from those we actually live in. Exchange, prices and social forces have a dominant impact on our beliefs and wants. This is particularly striking in asset markets – markets for houses, stocks and bonds – but is true far more generally. Beliefs are formed by groups as much as individuals. We learn by copying the behaviour of others. Copying and sharing views creates an implicit allegiance. It is also a form of insurance. If you think for yourself, you alone are to blame.

Over two thousand years ago, Aristotle drew a dividing line between the uses of money that are "necessary and approved of" and those uses for which it was not invented and are "justly regarded with disapproval" (*Politics* I258a38). This distinction remains relevant. Many of the unintended consequences of money are pernicious, such as its effects on our self-esteem, status and how we value and treat others. But Aristotle's understanding of the uses of money and finance was limited, like most people's. He provides an early example of confused and prejudicial views of debt, because he failed to identify its function and usefulness. Furthermore, it is not the case that all the unforeseen effects of money are destructive. Its most profoundly benign consequences are hard to discern in its basic purpose.

Economics offers a narrow description of money's functions: a store of wealth, a unit of account and a medium of exchange. The phrase "medium of exchange" is a dramatic understatement of why we primarily care about money. We engage in exchange to fulfil our needs, to provide for ourselves and our families. This is why most of the world is preoccupied with money. This is the primary function of money, which Aristotle calls "necessary". It explains money's essential purpose, but little else. It tells us nothing about how money can create peaceful societies and inter-generational ties, permit risk-taking, dominate our sense of status or cause manias and panics. To explain these effects I shall look at four philosophical properties of money: interdependence, control of the future, measurement and allure.

Interdependence is perhaps the most important property of money. Money is valueless unless it is recognized and accepted by others. It is a social contract, perhaps *the* social contract of modern societies. The division of labour, systems of finance and trade – complex, detailed, relationships between people – depend on money. Through their effects on our productivity, they free us from scarcity. Throughout the evolution of human organization, from family-based clans of hunter-gatherers to contemporary market democracies, caring for others requires a surplus of resources: some form of saving. A surplus must exist at an individual or collective level to provide for those who are in need or unlucky. The anthropological origins of money and credit are acts of sharing and care. Finance provides a formal substitute for many of the functions that were provided by extended families and clans in the past, which is equally essential in large and complex societies.

But exchange does not just create a surplus; it mediates where historically there was conflict. Markets and money provide an alternative to war and violence in our interaction with strangers, other tribes and cultures. War and conflict are often triggered by competing demands on scarce resources, and waged against those we do not know or do not like. It is surely preferable to determine the distribution of scare resources using prices rather than violence. Money, finance and trade have created an unprecedented level of interdependence between individuals and across nations. We now depend on others whom we may not like and, because our interests are mutual and overlap, we have an incentive to cooperate with them, however impersonally.

Money evolved from the institutions of gift exchange that prevail in simple tribal societies. These rituals serve an economic function of exchange, but are reciprocal and unite groups. Money fulfils an equivalent function in the highly complex division of labour that exists globally. The "gift" that creates an incentive for solidarity between the two most powerful nations in the world, China and the US, is the exchange of Chinese exports for US government bonds. Inevitably, as social organization has grown in scale and complexity, we have lost much of the affirmation of personal friendship and allegiance that is essential to original rituals of gift exchange, but money connects us and renders our interests mutual and over-lapping to an unprecedented degree. We depend more than ever before on those we do not know.

Money is unique within the institutional structure of our societies because it fulfils a similar role nationally and internationally. This is different from the law. Within most democratic nations, everyone is equally subject to the law. National law is fair because it is enforced by an independent authority. International law lacks independent enforcement, so it becomes an instrument for the powerful, and loses legitimacy. There is no such national boundary in our system of money and finance. Wherever the international division of labour, trade and finance goes, it extends our interdependence. But highly complex interdependence is also a precondition for correlated economic instability. This is not difficult to avoid and mitigate, but it requires a better understanding of both money and our attitudes towards it.

The least obvious function of money is *control of the future*. We strive to reduce uncertainty in our lives. Life is unliveable if we act and reason in a manner wholly consistent with the truth of how little we know. The future is particularly uncertain, and fraught with risk. Money is the means by which we try to control it. But this property is also paradoxical: human beings crave certainty, but are excited by risk. Money fulfils this desire benignly through inventive and experimental risk-taking, but also facilitates leveraged gambling. Surprisingly, it is this relationship to uncertainty and risk that money shares with religion. Religion also seeks to satisfy these desires. At times it provides the promise of certainty about our purpose or future, but it also pursues the intrinsic appeal of mystery and risk-taking.

The third property of money is *measurement*. This is necessary for money's original purpose – accounting and exchange – but it corrupts and confuses. Money measures some things very accurately, such as supermarket sales and balance sheets, and insidiously intrudes to measure others: such as status, perceptions of well-being or happiness. We try to measure things that cannot be measured, such as risk, and we distort the measurement of many others, such as the value of human endeavour.

The fourth property of money is its *allure*. Money's attraction is hard to pin down. It is not aesthetic, and cannot be explained just by money's usefulness. It is surely a consequence of all of money's properties, but also something independent.

The enabling and cooperative functions of money are more relevant than ever, but this underlying purpose is often hidden and is not what preoccupies us. When we think about money it is usually with concern; we associate money with worry, status, greed, materialism, financial instability and recession. Many of the adverse effects of money and markets are addressed, however imperfectly, through the tax system and regulation. But we also need to change our beliefs. Our confusion over the purpose of debt, saving, trade and exchange contributes to many of our anxieties and errors, and to our counterproductive behaviour. A failure of understanding explains why the policy response to recessions remains weak and confused. Recessions should end more quickly and impose little cost.

A full understanding of money's capacity to cause social instability and social progress requires awareness of how these four properties of money – interdependence, control of the future, measurement and allure – affect us all as individuals and collectively. But before we examine these properties in more detail we shall need a clear sense of exactly what money is and where it comes from. The ease with which money is both created and destroyed is itself intriguing. Money's origins help explain its capacity to destabilize, but also why it is remarkably easy to calm a panic; too easy, it seems. We shall try to identify why there is such a strong resistance to pursue very straightforward and costless solutions to financial panic and recession. For some reason, we fail to act rationally at great cost to ourselves and others.

1. Print it

It values everything, but costs nothing.

Child's play

Where money comes from is unknown to most people, including most who work in the world's financial centres. If you asked most finance ministers where money comes from they would be loath to admit to the truth: that they are not really sure. People rarely think about it. Like many things in life, using money doesn't usually require any understanding of how it works or even where it comes from. My young daughter is no different. She would prefer it if I was a policeman. "Hedge fund manager" doesn't mean much to her. But our system of money and banking has one property that intrigues even young and impatient minds: it functions mysteriously, almost magically; its origins are clandestine. The banking system is usually stable and disregarded, even though it ties all our activity together. It is intrinsically fragile because it depends on confidence, although no one is really conscious of this. Most mysteriously of all, when destabilized by panic – our sudden awareness of this fragility – it is usually costless to stabilize, requiring little more than pressing a button on a keyboard and speaking a few words. That is why it is easier to explain money's origins to children: it is too simple for adults to accept.

My daughter likes magic and mystery, so I try explaining banking to her. I leave hedge funds for another occasion, when I can think of a way to cast them in a positive light. Banks are useful. We deposit money with them, and they use this money to lend to other people, allowing them to buy houses or cars, and sometimes to pay bills. People need to borrow because houses and cars cost a lot and they cannot pay for them in one go. People also need to save. Banking is a kind of inter-temporal sharing arrangement: sharing across time. Some people have surplus money today, but they will need it in the future when they retire, others would like to borrow now and repay through time. It follows that savers are usually older than borrowers. Savers receive interest because they are lending money. A younger person gets a house, and an older one receives interest on their savings. Some countries seem to have higher interest rates than others. One reason is the age of the population. Countries with young populations are likely to have higher interest rates than those with older populations.

It doesn't take long to get into philosophy. My daughter's ability to reason is at the point where she can ask, "If God made us, who made God?" In a similar vein she asks me, "Where does the money come from, in the first place?" As with God, the origins of money are disconcerting when exposed to very straightforward scrutiny.

"What? They just *print it*?"

"Well ... actually, yes. In fact, they don't even have to bother printing it any more; they just press the 1 on their computer keyboard, and then the 0 a few times. They probably ask someone else to phys-ically press the keys, and there is almost certainly someone who checks that they don't make any mistakes ... Some central banks store some gold, just in case, and not very much. They hold gold mainly out of nostalgia for the era of metal standards when, say, one pound note could be exchanged for a pound of silver."

It is worth being clear about this process, because children are not alone in finding it disconcerting. I find it disconcerting, although I don't know why. This strange fear, engendered by our ability to create money out of nothing, explains in large part why governments and policy-makers have been so reluctant to prevent the needless economic suffering that is generated by financial panic. The fear is not completely irrational, as we shall see, but in the main it is. If the eurozone ever does break up, this irrationality will be the root cause.

Every year a country's central bank decides how much money to create, say, $1bn (or the local currency equivalent). They do not just gift this to the public, although they probably should. They usually get the money into the system by buying something from banks: usually government bonds. Over time, the amount of money in the economy grows depending on how much the central bank decides to create. They usually decide this on the basis of how fast they believe the economy can grow, and they grow the stock of money proportionately. This is entirely sensible. It happens all the time, and we pay no attention to it.

This real-world alchemy does not end with the central bank creating money out of thin air. Effortlessly, the banking system amplifies and multiplies the effects of this $1bn through lending. Banks lend the $1bn of cash they receive from the central bank to companies and individuals. Companies and individuals spend the money, paying other companies and individuals, who in turn deposit the money back in the bank, which lends it again, and so on. At the end of this multiplying process of lending, spending and re-depositing, deposits and loans grow to a multiple of the amount of money that the central bank created in the first place. Some people have savings, and other have houses: not just houses, of course, but factories, roads, universities and businesses.

It all happens without our really being aware that it happens. Progress depends on it. But we don't learn about it at school. It doesn't even get explained on business courses or in economics lessons. Many people believe that their money is stored in a safe at the bank, if they think about it at all. Ignorantly, we think of a deposit with a bank as money; indeed, in most of economics deposits are referred to as "money", and are categorized as such in official statistics, which is misleading. Deposits are not money: they are loans we make *to* banks.

This fact is essential to a banking panic. Precisely because the total value of deposits exceeds the amount of money in banks by a factor of twenty to thirty, if everyone tries to redeem their deposits at the same time the bank runs out of cash. But the solution to a banking panic is effortless, and disconcerting: a central bank merely needs to say that it will create as much money as is needed, and provide this to the banks, and everyone should calm down. If everyone wants to withdraw their deposits simultaneously, they can. If they can, they don't need to, so they won't. The central bank can provide this commitment as long as its computers are switched on. The banking system is stabilized instantaneously when there is trust, and the ability to create money at will creates this trust.

On 10 October 2008 we came very close to having a bank run across the entire global banking and financial system. We were lucky it was a Friday. Over the following weekend, the major countries of the world announced that they were willing to create as much money as was necessary should everyone wish to take out their deposits – they didn't use those precise words, but that was the implication – and so it was not necessary. It was too late to avoid the ensuing recession, caused in the main by the effects of this severe panic, but total collapse was averted. It cost nothing but words.

Too easy

You may not believe all of this, particularly if you are a normal, sensible person. It can't be that easy to prevent human suffering. Indeed, Franklin D. Roosevelt, US president during the later years of the Great Depression, is believed to have initially dismissed this solution, or a variant of it, precisely for being "too easy". For some reason, human beings are very resistant to the belief that something as important as money can be created so easily, and at no cost, and furthermore that during a panic, and a severe recession induced by the panic, money should be printed and handed out to the public to spend. There is nothing dangerous or irresponsible about this, no more than it is dangerous or irresponsible to use water to put out a fire.

I expect that you distrust this author's recommendation that a costless gift of cash to the public can ever solve serious economic problems. You may be inclined to check my credentials. Is the author a crank? It is human to seek reassurance from authoritative figures. We are all conventional. So I refer you to an article published by the current chairman of the US Federal Reserve Board, Ben Bernanke, perhaps the most powerful single policy-maker in the world. It is inelegantly entitled "Japanese Monetary Policy: A Case of Self-Induced Paralysis?" (Bernanke 2000). This paper was written by Bernanke when he was a professor at Princeton University in December 1999. He was unimportant then and could talk more openly and freely than he does now that his every word is scrutinized. In the paper, his final policy recommendation for Japan, which was perceived to be struggling with an apparently interminable recession, is precisely that the central bank print money and give it to the population. He was right, but they never did it. Why? Partly because they did not believe a solution could be that easy. And partly because they were scared.

What is the cause of this fear? Perhaps we are all hesitant and fearful in proximity to real power. There is a fine line between power and danger, and the authority to print money is an extraordinary power. The solution of simply printing money may seem trivial relative to the gravity of a recession, which incurs serious human suffering. It is nonsensical, irrational, but at least honest, to admit that you regard a solution as "too easy", as though to be credible in a crisis the measures must be difficult to take. Many of these attitudes are failures of analysis and understanding. This is not to say that extreme caution and vigilance are not warranted in granting power over the printing press, because in human history this power has been abused to very costly effect, generating rising inflation or *in extremis* hyperinflation.

How is it that money has these dual powers: to facilitate complex exchange and stave off panic in an instant, but also, in the wrong hands, to wreak its own destruction? The economist Paul Krugman makes frequent reference to an article in the *Journal of Money, Credit and Banking* by academics Joan Sweeney and Richard Sweeney (1977). The article analyses a babysitting group. I first came across this parable in Krugman's book *Peddling Prosperity* (1994), and despite the relatively trivial activity under study, it provides a uniquely clear way of answering this question.

A simplified version of the Sweeneys' story goes as follows. A large group of parents, mostly lawyers, decide to organize their babysitting requirements. It was probably one particularly high-powered couple who came up with the idea, and decided to impose it on the group (this is not a premise of the original paper, I should add). The parents decide to issue two "babysitting coupons" to each family, and things get off to a reasonable start. But after a month or so, parents try to save coupons and the system grinds to a halt. In an attempt to save and hold more than two coupons in reserve, everyone volunteers to babysit, and no one is willing to spend. There is a babysitting recession: a combination of unemployed babysitters, and no parents able to escape.

Being lawyers, their instinct is to legislate and force people to go out on predetermined days. But social events can't be legislated in advance. The strength of a *free* market is that it adapts to the specifics of time and place. Finally, after a lengthy consideration of Keynesian, Austrian and monetarist theories, they printed more coupons, and the babysitting economy recovered. That is exactly how money works in the economy. If everyone suddenly decides to save as much as they can – owing to panic, fear or extreme pessimism – activity will grind to a halt. The solution is to give them more money and assuage their fear.

Now imagine that the coupon-printing mother in the babysitting co-op starts to get greedy, and reasons that if she prints herself a few more coupons no one will notice. She tries a few times, and it works. So she does a few more. Soon, she goes a little mad and prints as many as she can. A problem then arises: more people want to go out than are willing to babysit. It does not take long for someone to start offering two coupons for one evening's babysitting. That's inflation. (If it continues, there will be a revolution, of course, and her trusted authority as the printer of coupons will be revoked.)

A country's level of inflation tells us a lot about that country. Normal levels of inflation, between 1 per cent and 5 per cent, imply that the institutions of government can function with a reasonable degree of trust, because the power to print money is not being abused. But if inflation goes from 5 per cent to 10 per cent, and then 30 per cent or higher, as is the case in Argentina or Zimbabwe, it tells you something more sinister is at work. For most of human history, sufficient trust did not exist for a system of paper money to persist. It is probably the case that sufficient trust *could not* exist, because there was no way to monitor rulers. That is why we relied on metal standards or used precious coins with intrinsic value. Our ability to monitor government, which requires information and independent institutions such as statistical agencies, legal institutions and a free press, has made paper and electronic money possible. Rapidly rising inflation is a sign of desperation, or dictatorship.

Retribution

We tend intuitively to think of many economic issues as zero-sum: one person's gain is another's loss. We find it difficult to accept that market economics works because, like most forms of human cooperation, the sum is worth more than the parts. But panic and fear impose costs on all of us because the process of cooperation breaks down. Printing money to stabilize a panic or reverse a recession benefits everyone at no necessary cost to anyone. Even many technical economists miss this point by perceiving the process purely in terms of inflation. This view is premised on the assumption that money is "neutral", meaning that it does not affect the level of economic activity, but only the price. But the parable of the babysitters illustrates otherwise. The availability of money in a panic directly affects the level of activity and not just the price, because contractions in the economy have enduring consequences. Money can defy the law of supply and demand. In very particular circumstances, if you produce more of it, its value (or purchasing power) can rise.

Severe recessions do not necessarily cause the price level to fall, but they are likely to permanently impair our ability to produce goods and services. In purely economic terms, recessions can result in a more sustained loss of skills and an irrecoverable loss of capital resources. This is enduring damage to what economists call the supply side of the economy: our ability to provide goods and services. At a more important human level recessions are likely to cause significant psychological scarring and, at their worst, increases in violence, crime and child poverty. The cold terminology of economics describes all of this as a decline in human or social "capital". All that really means is that it has enduring effects: it affects the future and not just the present.

For much of our economic history, and in many countries even now, such as Japan, the resistance to printing money during recessions is evident. We have identified the irrational fears. But there is another dimension to this opposition: retribution. A phase of growth, often a boom, usually precedes a panic or recession. And there are always high profile protagonists in any boom. The instinct for natural justice leads to the view that the recession brings just deserts to those protagonists; be they homeowners who "borrowed too much", high-tech firms that were over-optimistic, greedy bankers or irresponsible policy-makers. Many of these phrases are banal tautologies, particularly "greedy bankers", but more important than their accuracy is that they are of no relevance to how to respond to a panic or recession. The retributive point of view might be expressed as: let's needlessly incur a recession in which a great many people suffer because it may teach a reckless minority a lesson. But the ills of severe recession do not fall in any way fairly, nor does anyone learn any lessons. There is plenty of risk in life without us wilfully creating more. Wrongdoing should be punished in good times and bad; this is a separate matter. The belief that recessions are "cleansing" is a primitive and ignorant myth, more likely residing in a reflex desire for retribution than an understanding of economics or social change.

Printing money is costless. This can be the saviour of society, or its ruin. The fact that money is physically valueless remains disconcerting to many people, despite the huge facilitation of social organization and exchange that electronic money permits. Such is his unhappiness with this state of affairs that Texas Congressman Ron Paul recommends returning to the gold standard. He is convinced that the printing press is the root of all ills. A philosophical tension lies at the heart of this unease. The value of money is not physical, it is social. But we do not think of money's worth as residing in its social acceptance and trust in our institutions. Nor do we like the idea that people don't always get what they "deserve". We associate money with individualism, with selfishness, with materialism and miserliness, but the dependence of its value on institutional trust and its inherent social character is closer to something at the other extreme of human experience: morality.

2. Money's morality

To trade, the first condition was to be able to lay aside the
spear.   (Marcel Mauss, *The Gift*, [1954] 2008)

The great student of capitalism Karl Marx quotes approvingly from
Shakespeare's *Timon of Athens*:

Gold? Yellow, glittering, precious gold?

…

… much of this will make black, white; foul, fair;
Wrong, right; base, noble; old, young; coward, valiant.

…

This yellow slave
Will knit and break religions; bless th'accurst;
Make the hoar leprosy ador'd; place thieves,
And give them title, knee, and approbation,
With senators on the bench.

                (*The Life of Timon of Athens* IV.3,
                quoted in Marx [1956] 1986: 181)

Shakespeare describes how wealth and money – "gold" – alter our
attitude towards others. He believes in money's reflexive power:
it is not under our control; it affects us. But Shakespeare is not
moralizing, as Marx wants to imply. The conventional attitudes of
his time towards lepers and thieves were hardly noble. He reveals
our hypocrisy, and he observes that money reveals it too. Marx

is an insightful and stirring writer himself, although his argument often cedes to rhetoric. Like any great thinker struggling with original thoughts, he is particularly interesting when self-contradictory. He is critical, and ambiguous. His comment on this excerpt from Shakespeare is very revealing: "It [money] is the visible deity, the transformation of all human and natural qualities into their opposite, the universal confusion and inversion of things; *it brings incompatibles into fraternity*" ([1956] 1986: 181, emphasis added).

Marx sounds good but says nothing when he talks of "the transformation of all ... into their opposite". Why "opposite"? This is pure rhetoric. But he is right when he says money brings "incompatibles into fraternity". This is arguably the challenge of a free society: people who don't like each other – incompatibles – need to cooperate. No society, certainly no world, is likely to be homogeneous. Outside narrow family structures, most societies contain individuals and groups with competing objectives, wants and beliefs about how to live their lives. The need to create "fraternity" between those who do not have familial ties is a prerequisite for peaceful and voluntary forms of social organization.

This function of money is clearer when we look at the forms of social and political organization that precede it. Money and trade evolved alongside independent legal institutions as a means of conflict resolution. In *Guns, Germs and Steel*, Jared Diamond describes the pattern of political evolution in New Guinea from bands of hunter-gatherers to tribes, and then to chiefdoms of several hundred people. It is a process of evolving forms of conflict resolution, as social organization moves further away from the extended family or clan:

> One reason why the organisation of human government tends to change from that of a tribe to a chiefdom in societies with more than a few hundred members is that the difficult issue of conflict resolution between strangers becomes increasingly acute in larger groups. (1997: 271)

In social evolution, morality starts in the family. But it is striking that tribes with very strong moral bonds *within* their close-knit group – often distributing resources according to need or straightforward egalitarian principles – can engage in brutal and violent conflict with other groups when they perceive a threat or conflict of interest. The very same people are highly moral and appallingly immoral in their regard for others. Within family structures obligations (or debts) towards older members of the family are informal and taken for granted, as is care of the unfortunate, such as children whose parents die or are killed. As the numbers of the clan increase, the means of mediating conflict and creating bonds becomes less familial and, even when distribution remains egalitarian, informal obligations play an increasing role: "no member of a traditional tribe can become disproportionately wealthy by his or her own efforts, because each individual has debts and obligations to many others" (*ibid.*: 272).

Disputes *within* clans are settled non-violently through agreements negotiated within family structures. The major problem that emerges is how to settle disputes over resources *between* clans, if the family structure is the sole means of regulation. Violent solutions are typical. Even where complex rituals of gift-giving evolve to exchange goods between clans with structured forms of reciprocity and even "interest", the solidarity is extremely fragile. In his classic study of tribal gift-exchanges, the anthropologist Marcel Mauss describes how tribes suddenly pass from festivals full of reciprocity to battle, "substituting alliance, gifts and trade, for war isolation and stagnation". He is highly suggestive of the moral progress implied by exchange and trade:

> Two groups of men who meet can only either draw apart, and, if they show mistrust toward one another or issue a challenge, fight – or they can negotiate. Until legal systems and economies evolved … it is always with strangers that one "deals".
>
> ([1954] 2008: 105)

Difference is often a source of hostility between people, but it is the premise of mutually beneficial trade. Shakespeare observes how status or social hierarchy can be subverted by money, which is something we shall return to. But there is a deeper sense in which trade transforms our attitude towards strangers: economic opportunity. The benefits of exchange and trade reside in differences in skills, technology, culture, practices and natural resources.

This point is often made using David Ricardo's concept of comparative advantage, which shows how under certain conditions trade between countries or regions is beneficial even if one country is better at producing all goods. Comparative advantage is clever and counter-intuitive, but rarely relevant. Far more important is the ability of trade and exchange to transform the relationship between tribes into a relationship of opportunity (and possibly friendship), and the very broad nature of that opportunity. Comparative advantage simply points to the potential benefits of specialization, subject to a great many assumptions that often do not hold. What is far harder to dispute is that general openness to trade and exchange across countries, regions, societies and cultures, and particularly the exchange of ideas, in the broadest sense, is immensely beneficial.

Other countries, strangers, have not just natural resources that we may not have, but also novel ways of making things, of organizing businesses, institutions and legal systems. The exchange of independently developed technologies has been central to economic development. In his economic history *The Wealth and Poverty of Nations,* David Landes illustrates how the development of ideas, and their application, is contingent on circumstance. Progress is often gained through trade in ideas: through copying, applying or combining the ideas of others in different conditions. Economic, social and political development relies on openness. The failure of Chinese technology to progress relative to Western Europe, given China's vastly superior starting position as early as the eleventh century, is a case in point. China is believed to have used coal in blast furnaces for smelting seven hundred years prior to Britain. The Chinese had a water-driven machine for spinning hemp in the twelfth century, five hundred years before England's industrial revolution. But this lead was soon lost: "One generally assumes that knowledge and know-how are cumulative; surely a superior technique, once known, will replace older methods. But Chinese industrial history offers examples of technological oblivion and regression" (Landes 2002: 55).

Why did China experience technological regression? There are probably multiple reasons, but opposition to internal free exchange, cross-border trade and the diminished contact with the practice and applications of ideas by others are significant. Under the Ming Dynasty (1368–1644) the state attempted to prohibit all overseas trade. Maritime trade was viewed as a diversion from imperial concerns. Determined aggressors will resist laying down the spear and spurn the mutual benefits of trade.

Mutual dependence

Exchange precedes money in social evolution, but money vastly expands the scope and complexity of exchange and the division of labour. Money extends the division of labour across societies, countries and time. This process does not just work to our mutual benefit, but also increases our dependence on others. Exchange creates an incentive for us to consider their interests. The Scottish thinker David Hume, who was writing well before the artificial distinction between philosophy, economics and psychology became commonplace, describes the effects in *An Enquiry Concerning Human Understanding*:

The mutual dependence of men is so great in all societies that scarce any human action is entirely complete in itself, or is performed without some reference to the actions of others, which are requisite to make it answer fully the intention of the agent. The poorest artificer, who labours alone, expects at least the protection of the magistrate, to ensure him the enjoyment of the fruits of his labour. He also expects that, when he carries his goods to market, and offers them at a reasonable price, he shall find purchasers, and shall be able, by the money he acquires, to engage others to supply him with those commodities which are requisite for his subsistence. In proportion as men extend their dealings, and render their intercourse with others more complicated, they always comprehend, in their schemes of life, a greater variety of voluntary actions, which they expect, from the proper motives, to co-operate with their own.   ([1777] 1989: 89)

Interdependence is the first philosophical property of money. Money is a social contract and its value depends on its recognition by others and the enforceability of property rights. Money's most essential function is to facilitate exchange and hence the division of labour. This creates a series of benefits. Exchange occurs because it is mutually beneficial. The division of labour increases our productivity, freeing us from scarcity and its associated aggression. Surplus is a precondition for care of others and the creation of independent institutions of law and government.

Many of the mutual benefits of trade in ideas, goods and services, occur precisely because those with whom we trade are different to us. Exchange transforms out attitudes towards strangers: we learn to view them as opportunities for trade, learning and innovation. In this way money has helped transform social organization from familial structures of distribution and regulation into large populous nations with formal and objective institutions.

Character

Within developed countries conflicts between families and clans are rarely settled through brutal conflict. Money, exchange and the division of labour have helped create more peaceful societies. But are we better individuals?

Cognitive psychologists use the term "heuristic" to describe various devices that we use to reason under conditions of complexity. We don't have the mental capacity or information to fully think through most things in a rational or calculated fashion, so we have evolved with many short cuts, rules of thumb and concepts that help us to function. *Character* is a heuristic of moral reasoning. It is a rule of thumb for predicting how people might behave in unknown future circumstances. Moral decision-making becomes increasingly complex and difficult when the implications involve the behaviour of others in the future. Often we are not present when decisions that matter to us are being made; we have to trust others. Character is the moral equivalent of reputation in business. Game theory shows that moral character, like reputation, can be functional in repeated games (Binmore 2005). This does not mean that people of good character are ultimately selfish; by definition they are not. But it may explain why they survive, and why their societies are more likely to survive. People of good character act morally: they give consideration to the interests of all affected by their actions. They also care about themselves and others in the future.

Although motives are often irrelevant to the assessment of the appropriateness of an action or decision, they do reveal character and so are important in our expectations about how people will behave in differing circumstances and in the future. Most of the time we behave morally, but our motives are often unclear because it is also in our interest to act morally. We do not know if character is inherited, learnt, acquired through habit or influenced by incentives and the behaviour of others. My guess is that all these factors matter.

How does money alter character? When you work in a financial centre, such as London or New York, most of your social life occurs on the commuter train. This is testimony to the quiet victory of effort over thought. Independent and perceptive thinking is not prioritized or valued in contemporary occupations, even in those where it is the most valuable skill. The collective tendency towards conventional, measurable behaviour has resulted in an increased emphasis on being seen to be at the office or at the desk. Thought has diminished in quality and quantity, and so has life outside work.

But commuting is occasionally interesting. Several months ago, taking the train to work in the City, I witnessed a pregnant woman sitting on the carriage floor. No one was willing to give up their seat. I was already standing, and not in a position to offer direct assistance. At a guess, about eight of the twelve seats were occupied by well-dressed men, all sitting comfortably and apparently unperturbed. Matters then got worse: these affluent and able-bodied professionals looked on while another pregnant woman in the carriage offered *her* seat to the more-pregnant woman, who was clearly in distress. I had never before witnessed anything similar, but on this occasion my journey was somewhat unusual: I was travelling in first class. This begs the obvious question: are rich people wankers? Or, to put it more philosophically, does wealth erode our character?

It should not. Moral behaviour is defined by care for others, or at least consideration of their interests. This is universal to all moral systems. Regardless of nationality, culture or religious belief, any reasonable person can understand why there is an obligation to give up one's seat on a train for a pregnant woman. The main forms of care for others in societies – care for children, the elderly or the unfortunate – require an excess of resources. So a surplus of resources is a precondition for moral behaviour. The rich start from a position of strength: care for others does not involve much sacrifice.

Poverty appears a more reasonable justification for immoral endeavour. If the degree of surplus defines our moral potential, scarcity defines its limits. Extreme scarcity is characterized by situations of *direct* conflict of interest. A direct conflict of interest is a situation where competing interests are mutually exclusive: the benefits or costs cannot be shared. In the extreme, one person's survival depends on another's death. Direct conflicts of interest preclude moral action, unless one of the competing interests clearly outweighs the others.

Much of recent moral philosophy centres around so-called moral dilemmas. Their structure is usually the same: clear cases of direct conflict of interest where one interest does not outweigh the other, and therefore there is no morally determined course of action. When there is a direct conflict of interest, morality only prescribes a definitive course of action if one interest very clearly outweighs the other: such as a pregnant woman's discomfort and potential health risk from standing, relative to the modest discomfort of an able-bodied man. Conflicts of interest create an incentive for immoral or amoral behaviour: immoral if the right thing to do is clear but at odds with self-interest, amoral if there is a direct conflict of interest and neither interest has greater weight. A war for survival, if there is insufficient food to feed both factions, is amoral. A war to increase resources beyond subsistence is immoral. When resources are scarce, direct conflicts of interest are ambiguous. Consider a more relevant example: is it wrong for a low-skilled self-employed worker to avoid taxes if the income he saves improves the health and education of his children?

As a generic observation about societies, it does appear to be the case that the greater the surplus of resources the more moral the society is, at least internally. Developed countries tend to have better human rights records, lower crime rates, better health care, better social security and care of the elderly than developing countries. Rich countries have formal institutions that provide these services to all citizens, in contrast to the entirely intra-family informal arrangements of hunter-gatherer or tribal societies.

But something is not quite right in this description of our moral progress. A scene such as the one I witnessed on the train is unimaginable in the Dublin I grew up in the 1970s, although it was a far poorer community than the commuter belt around London. So there is a paradox: we have better societies but our character does not seem enhanced. Why has character been left behind by progress? Money impacts our character in three ways. First, through incentives. Incentives that align our own interests with those of others are *moral incentives.* Punishment serves to align self-interest with what is "right", by creating an incentive to obey the law (assuming that the law is right). Mutual benefit works in the opposite direction to scarcity and creates a moral incentive, which is independent of punishment or retribution. Money's most basic function is to facilitate the exchange of goods and services and the division of labour. The prevalent motivation for engaging in free exchange is that both parties perceive it to be in their interests. If social cooperation is mutually beneficial we have an incentive to care for others. Their interests become ours.

The second effect of money on our character is more pernicious: money seems to alter our perceptions of our own needs. It is true that progress creates new "needs". New pharmaceutical drugs or medical operations or technology to control the environment might fit this description. But accumulating money and resources does not seem to diminish our desire to *acquire.* Mimetic social competition is too strong a motivation. Hume argues that property rights and the rule of law are required owing to scarce resources. "For what purpose make a partition of goods, when everybody has already more than enough?", he asks ([1777] 1989: 184). Today, he might rethink the apparent self-evidence of this claim. Our desire to acquire is not easily satiated, or at least requires self-awareness and conscious control. We have generated huge surpluses of resources, way beyond what we need to survive, but our perception of what is required to live a decent life seems to be determined by our income, and to increase accordingly (Layard 2006: 49). We don't believe we have excess resources, despite evidence to the contrary. The social and economic system's ability to create the perception of limitless "need" may in part explain why rich nations are not more generous. It is difficult otherwise to explain our failure to follow the economically rigorous and politically pragmatic advice of Jeffrey Sachs, who estimates that a Marshall Plan for Africa would cost less than 1 per cent of the developed world's GDP (Sachs 2005). Sachs may of course be wrong about our ability to affect the welfare of other countries, but why not try? The cost is trivial.

The third effect of money on our character is the illusion of independence. When discussing Thomas Hobbes in *The Wealth of Nations*, Adam Smith describes money and wealth as power over the labour of others ([1776] 1999: 134). The labour of others is required for many of the things we want and need, although not all. But power is still a form of interdependence, albeit one that is imbalanced. Great imbalances of wealth and income do translate into imbalances of power, to varying degrees and often in complex and non-linear ways. But it is a mistake to interpret this as independence; sudden loss of wealth or other forms of power tend to make this abruptly clear. You can sense this in politicians after they have left office. They never quite recover; often they appear somewhat pathetic. *Do you know who I am?* Often the correct answer is: "Yes, I do; and right now you need my cooperation."

The character of rich individuals is corrupted not by scarcity, but by a naive sense of independence, and by social competition for esteem, which creates wants sometimes absurdly in excess of need. Naivety explains the pathos in the fall from grace of the once-powerful chief executive officer (CEO). Human beings who have been lucky often confuse this with skill. The rich have been lucky. As Paul Samuelson says, "If you are so rich, why are you so dumb?" (2005).

Does the illusion of independence and a distorted sense of superiority explain the behaviour in the first class carriage on my commute? Since writing the original draft of this chapter, I have paid closer attention to the travellers in first class. Based on their reading material I have come to the conclusion that most of them are not rich people at all, but civil servants. Perhaps bureaucratic power is more corrupting of character than money.

Complex exchange

So money's impact on human behaviour and organization is more ambivalent than we might assume. Money lacks intrinsic value, and it requires social acceptance and trust in the institutions that control it. We tend to think of money as corrupting and corrosive, particularly when we think of its effects on character, and there is truth in this, but money's primary functions expand our reliance on others. Money enters social evolution as a means of conflict resolution and, by facilitating trade, it transforms our relationships with those who are different from us. The surplus that follows from the higher productivity that the division of labour brings allows us to be moral towards others and towards ourselves and others in the future. He who only has the resources to survive can do neither.

Economics makes a very powerful observation that follows from free exchange: if the parties to trade are correct in perceiving the exchange to be beneficial to them, the very occurrence of exchange makes them collectively better off. This insight is often neglected. The exchange of second-hand goods on eBay means that the very same goods serve more people's needs, in this case without any increase in production. But the concept of mutual and collective benefit becomes far less straightforward than economic reasoning implies when we move beyond the trade and exchange of essential goods and services, as Aristotle suggested. Standard economics assumes that what we want is in our interests (who is best placed to make that judgement is another issue again); that our needs and wants are given, and not determined or influenced by the process of exchange itself; and that our preferences are consistent. All three of these assumptions must hold for the process of exchange to be of certain mutual benefit. (For exchange to be *collectively* beneficial, we need to add a fourth assumption: that there are no negative "externalities", that is, negative effects or costs of exchange that are not borne by the parties to exchange. Pollution is the textbook example of an externality.) But in reality there is a reflexive relationship between our beliefs and wants and the process of exchange. It is the source of many of money's adverse effects, a point the Marxian tradition has long emphasized, as more recently has the field of behavioural economics. Exchange *does* affect our perceptions of what we believe, our self-esteem and status, and what we aspire to have. Our wants are not given; they are influenced by what others have. This creates envy and social competition. We want what others have, and we think we need it.

Money's morality

Cormac McCarthy's novel *The Road* portrays the attempts of a father and son to survive in a world of extreme scarcity. They try to make their way across the wasteland: a future America devastated by some catastrophic explosion or ecological disaster. *The Road* can be read as a meditation on human behaviour under conditions of extreme scarcity. It reveals our moral intuitions through a story. At one point, the father and son search a long beach for things that may be of use, and leave their shopping cart, which contains all their belongings, at their makeshift camp, unguarded. On return, they discover that all their belongings have been stolen, including the shoes of the father and son. To survive, but also motivated by anger, they hunt down the perpetrator. When they confront him and demand their things, he pulls out a knife. The father, incensed, has a gun, and threatens to kill the man unless he returns the entire contents of their trolley. But now, out of moral indignation and a desire for retribution he also demands that the thief turn over all of his own belongings too. Afterwards his son is upset. The father reassures him and says that he had no intention of shooting the man. But the son knows that in all likelihood the thief will die anyway, as he now has no belongings. After prolonged consideration and discussion, the father relents. They return the thief's possessions.

This story is very revealing. The father's reaction is in part a response to his perception of the thief's character: he stole knowing he would endanger the life of a child. Now, was the retribution the father sought for this revelation of character an appropriate response? The son did not think so. He may have empathized with the thief. Indeed, he says to his father: "He was just hungry, Papa. He was going to die." He may also have been concerned by the small, but not zero, probability that the thief survives and seeks revenge.

The father's initial decision was instinctive. Our instincts have evolved in conditions of scarcity and are plausibly functional in these conditions. Was he right to allow the thief to survive? Character is a device we use to assess prospective behaviour in circumstances we cannot predict or know about now, an accurate description of much of life. How would the thief behave if he encounters another father and child, and another opportunity to steal?

Earlier in the novel, McCarthy subtly reveals the social character of money: its dependence on cooperation and social institutions. The father and son happen upon a solitary house in a field, which they scavenge for useful items. The father finds a double handful of gold Krugerrands in a cloth sack. But he leaves them behind. He didn't find what he was looking for, something far more useful than money in a lawless world: "There was no gun and there wasn't going to be one".

3. Global money

[The free market] draws all, even the most barbarian, nations into civilisation. The cheap prices of its commodities are the heavy artillery with which it batters down all Chinese walls, with which it forces the barbarians' intensely obstinate hatred of foreigners to capitulate.   (Karl Marx & Friedrich Engels, *The Communist Manifesto*, [1872] 1985: 81–5)

Nationalism

If people believe in something it is true. This is generally incorrect, but perhaps not in the case of national identity. The concept of national identity usually implies that people of that nation have something in common. Some Irish people believe their identity is defined by what they have in common with others born in Ireland, which creates a deep allegiance. I struggle with this, perhaps because one side of my family are immigrants from Italy. But I have always been conscious of what makes you fit in, why some people get on well with others and, in a similar but different vein, what makes people cooperate. Do you need to be similar to another person to be at ease with them, to cooperate or enjoy their company?

Another source of scepticism about national identity is logical and empirical: opposite sides in Northern Ireland have more in common with each other than they do with anyone else in the world. Most people do not even understand the language of their dispute: the symbolic and cultural significance of marches, types of music and songs, arcane interpretations of religious rites. The Northern Irish have a great deal in common, and yet their animosity is violent and extreme. Civil wars and family feuds epitomize the coexistence of cultural commonality and antagonism.

Groups *do* like superficial similarities. If you wear the same clothes, profess to like similar music or adhere to a political ideology you are on the same side. Copying, mimetic behaviour, is not just the means by which we learn, but also an expression of allegiance. But saying "I am on your side" is not the same as saying "we are the same", or "we have a lot in common". In Northern Ireland, the people have a great deal in common, and use signals, which are incoherent to the outsider, to express the opposite: *you are not on my side*. The simplest forms of group association make this distinction between being on the same side and sharing an identity, or having a great deal in common, more explicit. Football fans of different clubs in Manchester are culturally almost identical, and yet on opposite sides (Brown 2002). In contrast, many fans of London clubs have nothing cultural in common with other supporters of the same club and yet they are on the same side.

An Irish friend I grew up with had very few friends when we lived in Dublin; he was a bit of a misfit. He tended not to like many other people. Years later we had both moved to London and met up for a drink. The man who had disliked most Irish people when he lived in Ireland had now become super-Irish. Even his accent seemed more pronounced. He had joined Irish societies in London and he socialized predominantly with Irish people.

Nationalism is premised on a myth, and a truth. The myth is that the people of a nation are bound together by some great shared experience or culture; the truth is that they are on the same side if they believe in the myth. But the comfort derived from identifying with a group, often only in our minds, is very important to our thinking and decision-making. In finance, as in life, we often do foolish things simply because others in our group are doing them.

No dogma

To feel most comfortable, in friendship, you need to feel you are on the same side. This is primal. Cooperation is less demanding than friendship. To cooperate you only need to know the rules of the game; there don't have to be sides. It helps if the game is mutually beneficial. The German philosopher Walter Benjamin described capitalism as a unique religion because it has no *dogma*. Religions typically have a core set of indisputable tenets that a person must know in order to be a follower of that religion. But most people engaged in capitalism don't even realize that they are. Perhaps that is why it has spread universally.

Although there is no dogma of global capitalism, there are rules. The rules of markets and exchange are identifiable and, subject to the constraints of the law and international agreements, intrinsically voluntary. Implicitly, trade and exchange (of money, beliefs, technology, know-how) is perceived as mutually beneficial, although not always "fair". I shall return to this, but first it is worth reflecting on the achievement of a global system of money, because it is in many ways remarkable and unlikely.

We have seen that money's value is no longer intrinsic: it depends on its social acceptance; maintaining its value requires confidence in institutional continuity. We no longer steal other countries' gold. To exchange money, to engage in international finance and trade, we don't just need to trust our own government: we need to trust theirs. Most unpredictable of all, many people now trust the institutions of other countries more than they trust their own. Tribalism has been negated. Globalized money allows people to import institutional stability and continuity from other countries. The eurozone is an explicit case in point. Many countries, particularly now in central and eastern Europe, use the prospect of euro entry as a means of promoting institutional reform. Other countries import institutional stability from abroad, and bypass national governments. The Argentine government cannot provide its people with a future, but Argentines believe that the American government can, so they use dollars. All important financial decisions made by the middle class in Argentina – savings, mortgages – are transacted and denominated in dollars. The movement of capital allows those with access to it to import the perceived institutional stability of another country. It is equivalent to migration. Migration is often premised on the belief that the country of destination has better institutions than one's country of origin.

These are extreme examples, and there are important and possibly self-destructive aspects to these developments. But cross-border investment, finance and trade require trust in institutional and legal continuity. Global money and exchange create interdependence. As long as exchange is voluntary it must be perceived to be mutually beneficial, or it is unlikely to occur. The extent of our interdependence is often unrecognized. Money has brought not just incompatibles into fraternity, but unknowns into fraternity. Consider Taiwan. Most people in the world know virtually nothing about Taiwan. It is an extraordinary country: politically treacherous, as it claims independence from the People's Republic of China, and physically vulnerable, as it is susceptible to earthquakes. Unwittingly, we are more dependent today on Taiwan than on Arab oil. Around 60 per cent of the world's semiconductors are produced in Taiwan; this is a far greater market share of an essential component of the technology industry than Saudi Arabia's share of our global energy needs.

The globalization of money is highly imperfect: an evolution of the possible. Some have argued that globalization ends in war, others that it is not fair. It is certainly poorly understood, like money in general. Marx identifies a dual consequence of the division of labour. Once we leave a subsistence world, work becomes an intrinsically social activity. It involves cooperation. The division of labour involves greater cooperation and more interdependence than do more basic economic arrangements. But it can also remove the direct human interaction involved in simpler exchange, or other forms of human cooperation where human effort is not described as "work".

Once there is a market for work, our attitude towards our own work and those affected can change. This conflict between growing interdependence and less direct human contact is a recurrent theme in Marx's work. He was describing economies dominated by low-skilled manufacturing activity, which implies a very different form of social interaction from those prevalent in service-based or higher-skilled economies. But Marx still identifies a very contemporary experience: we are concerned about the treatment of labour in many low-skilled occupations in developing countries. We often know little about the conditions under which many goods we buy are produced, because we have no direct physical and social relationship with those involved. But at the same time the only reason there is any link at all is precisely because of the same division of labour. We become separated from some of our fellow men, but also connected to a great many more.

Will global money end in war?

Predicting a global war at some point in the future is hardly insightful. Human history is a record of repeated war, so it has to be reasonably probable that at some point in the future there will be another world war. I don't know what that probability is, but it is not zero. Hopefully it is very low. Does the globalization of money, trade and finance – the spread of global capitalism and free markets – make war more likely?

Some historians try to explain a sequence of events from the past with a theory, and on this basis to make predictions about the future. This is statistics with a sample of one; or at best, a sample of a few. It is story-telling with a great plot, but little insight. Facts and evidence from history can tell us much more than theories about why events occurred. Facts often show that the conventional wisdom about human behaviour, beliefs and organization is flawed or unoriginal. But theories about the future derived from history are laden with bias.

Niall Ferguson is a thought-provoking historian. He is at his best when he uses history as a mine of information about how human beings can behave. History is full of evidence that undermines our prejudices or illuminates our sense of human potential. He is at his worst when he is predicting. Ferguson (2005) puts forward the thesis that the current global economy resembles the previous great globalization, under British colonialism, which ended with the Second World War: a sample of one. Similarly pessimistic about today, he sees globalization ending in wars over limited natural resources. This is a popular apocalyptic vision: John Gray draws similar conclusions from the opposite end of the political spectrum in his *False Dawn* (2002).

Is the parallel with this era of "overstretched" British colonialism valid? We have seen how scarcity is the root of amorality. So Ferguson is right to view scarce resources as a potential source of conflict. Fair solutions are more difficult to find in a zero sum world: impossible if survival depends on consumption of these resources. But this has nothing to do with global capitalism and finance. Human beings are likely to have to share finite resources whatever system of economic and political organization they choose to adopt. But a global market economy stands a far better chance of peacefully coordinating the distribution of scarce resources, and encouraging our adaptation to life without them, than a polarized and disparate system would.

Markets do not just extend interdependence, bringing the fraternity of incompatibles across borders: the price mechanism also functions to allocate scarce resources. This remains very poorly understood. Higher energy prices provide the only way to coordinate the behaviour of the entire world to reduce its energy dependence. This is a truism. There is less likely to be a war over scarce resources if there is a market for these resources: as they become scarcer the price will rise, reducing dependency and encouraging innovation to substitute.

The exchange of ideas

The differences between today's globalization and that of historic empires are more striking than the similarities. To describe America's global influence as an *empire* is dramatic, but misleading. An empire relies on coercive power, and direct use of force. America uses military power at the periphery of the world economy (Afghanistan and Iraq are not economically significant) and, like all countries, America tries to use diplomatic coercion elsewhere. But none of this reflects America's power. Measured by their impact on the behaviour of others, these acts of force are of second-order significance. If anything they point to a weakness of American political structure and imagination. No, America's main influence has been to show others how to organize their society – politically and economically – not to force or control others directly.

The practical man who believes in realpolitik in fact has a naive view of power. So does the conventional politician. There is a striking inconsistency when politicians in the United Kingdom argue that Britain's influence would be greater if it were more directly engaged in Europe. Britain's influence is far greater where it does not engage, for example in monetary policy. Political negotiations, through international organizations, resemble crude barter, and are unlikely to result in long-lasting influence. The most effective way to change a person or a country's behaviour is to show them a more effective means to achieve their objectives. The power of example is far greater than that of diplomacy or military might. Examples and ideas change behaviour in permanent ways, because voluntary cooperation has many advantages over coercion, not least because more people are likely to be getting what they want, resources do not need to be diverted towards force and conflict, and local information is being utilized. Coercion is usually centralized. Today's globalization is unique because it is voluntary. The globalization of Britain's empire was forced. A voluntary system of interdependence is likely to be much more stable, and produce much better results, than a system of force.

It is not even accurate to describe the spread of free market capitalism and democracy as *American* influence, because these are not originally American ideas. Ancient Greece is the blueprint for the democratic model of political organization. Appropriately, the origin and evolution of market structures are less certain and more diffuse, perhaps Dutch or Chinese. But whoever invented the first market created an idea that has conquered the world: an example with extraordinary power; a religion with no dogma.

Should we all get the same amount?

The globalization of money and markets is a force for peace if it fosters voluntary interdependence. It coordinates without taking sides. This is not just to replace Ferguson's pessimistic sample-of-one story with an alternative optimistic story. There is plenty of scope for conflict, but markets don't provoke wars over scarce resources; they provide an alternative means of distribution. The stability of global interdependence that prevails is also fortuitous, because the absence of a competing ideology is a historical accident. Had Marxism never been tested before, now would be its coming of age. The progress of ideologies, like that of all ideas, is unpredictable (Popper [1957] 1991).

Interdependence alone is hardly enough to guarantee peace; it exists, after all, even between a slave and his master. The most obvious and valid criticism of markets is not the absence of interdependence, but the inequity of the distribution of wealth, income and opportunities that is produced. Marx is accurate in describing a fair or just distribution as "to each according to his needs". Typically, this is the rule of distribution that families follow. He observed, quite rightly, that this is not the distribution markets produce.

When viewed purely in terms of income and wealth it is interesting that the egalitarian criticism is a materialistic one. It assumes that our interests and needs are best defined in material terms. The pro-market tradition has taken a more philosophical or even spiritual view of our primary interests, emphasizing freedom and liberty. Friedrich Hayek's critique of communism and socialism is called *The Road to Serfdom*, not *The Road to Poverty*. Hayek's own view of the role of government is far less doctrinaire than that of many of his followers. Reading *The Road to Serfdom* today, it is striking how he recognizes the importance of government and planning, while defining its limitations by the complexity of the task at hand. He argues that the advantage of a complex, voluntary system of independence is not that it is fair, in the sense of producing an equal distribution, but that it avoids concentrations of power, accesses more information and coordinates this knowledge more effectively than a centrally planned system. Individuals in a free market use local and unique internal knowledge. Central planners do not have access to information that is unique, changing, internal to the human mind and particular to time and place. At the same time, planners require a centralization of power and initiative and the destruction of innovation. Communism was not, as Marx hoped, a means to self-realization, but the destruction of freedom.

Contingency

Within certain constraints, the distributional consequences of markets are random. Market systems coordinate exchange through prices. The consequences of this will be particular to time and place. Economic history suggests that well-organized market economies produce a surplus well beyond our essential needs at the aggregate, but the distribution of this surplus varies dramatically.

It is likely that all perspectives on social organization are necessarily contingent. This is another way of saying it depends on the circumstances. Hayek, as a vociferous advocate of free markets, tends to think of middle class Vienna full of skilled artisans, merchants and intellectuals, engaging in free exchange. Marx has brutal industrial Manchester in the mid to late 1800s in mind. Something similar to these two images probably co-exists in today's world, depending where you are. Capitalism has very different implications for people's lives depending on which country they live in, on their levels of skills and education, and on the specific form of capitalism that prevails where they are. This will change in the future.

The contingent nature of the problem is why more recent political theorists such as John Rawls have tended to define consideration of the optimal form of organization in terms of a principle, an ultimate rule of the game. Rawls is implicitly observing that even if a system of social organization, indeed any form of human coordination, may not be fair in each individual outcome, it can still be legitimate; if the rules of the game are fair and likely to have been agreed by all affected, assuming they are reasonable. Rawls concludes that the optimal social order maximizes the position of the least well off. This could be conceived of in terms of the society that the least well off would choose. Rawls suggests that this choice is made behind a veil of ignorance about one's prospective status.

I doubt such an approach is particularly useful. If you introduce the issues of time, future generations or future selves, risk and the choices we can make about having future generations, such reasoning rapidly becomes extremely complex and probably indeterminate: philosophy that is more akin to a logical puzzle, and about as useful. Human beings are adaptive and eclectic, because the world changes and different systems suit different conditions. In order to work successfully, centrally planned, collective, needs-oriented social organization needs to be relatively small and homogeneous, or dictatorial – like the family unit or village organization. At national and international levels, we need a system that coordinates incompatibles. So we use one system of distribution in the family and another in large complex societies. We try to mitigate the negative distributional effects of markets and the distorted incentive effects of government. We seek to encourage and strengthen the positive tendencies of both. Different countries, technologies, skills and institutions all produce differing results. What is important is not to structure some complex, artificial and probably impossible abstract choice, but to better understand what we have, what has worked and why.

The perceived conflict between central planning and the market system has been detrimental to the development of political ideas. One consequence Hayek observes is insufficient analysis of competing types of capitalism and the optimal organization of capitalism. I would say the same is true of government. Too many great minds devoted their energies to criticizing government instead of thinking about how to organize this essential institution more effectively. It is obvious that markets only function to serve us well if there is a well-planned framework in which they operate, and in many circumstances of human organization markets are inappropriate and their effects detrimental. Reflecting on the properties of money makes this duality obvious. Its value requires rules governing its use and issuance. This requires centralized institutions with regulated and legitimate power. But it serves to liberate us from necessity and to engage in highly creative, complex interaction and exchange with those we may not like, and often don't even know. Market-based systems have been adopted voluntarily by an increasing number of countries because they seem to work better than competing forms of large scale economic organization. It is conceivable that at some point in the future we will find a better way to coordinate complex and heterogeneous societies. Or maybe, some time in the future, society will be simpler, and people will all be the same. If there is such a future, it is very distant. In the meantime, global money and regulated markets will coordinate the behaviour of potential antagonists, usually to their mutual benefit.

4. Future selves, worry and *Schuld*

How easy is it to be selfish?

Recently, returning to my family home in Dublin, I discovered a photograph of myself aged nine or ten. I can remember the day it was taken. Someone had given me a simple inexpensive camera as a gift. On a late afternoon after school I took photographs of all the members of my family, and one of them must have taken one of me. It was probably my father. He always took the photographs in our family, so the ones I took that day are among the few we have of him.

The experiences of that child affect who I am today. I share memories with him. We share origins, and experiences. But he could easily have had a very different life from mine. Am I the same person as him? Some of the decisions I made as a child still influence me today. Decisions I make now may affect me, or my children, in twenty or thirty years' time. Distance, measured by time, presents our self in the past or future as another person. There is a tension between the self now and in the future that mirrors the conflicts that can exist between our interests and those of others. Everyday language reveals this tension: we do not always *do ourselves justice*. The colloquial phrase "look after yourself", a phrase the Irish use a lot, suggests that often we do not. This is not impractical or irrelevant philosophy: when I wake in the morning with a severe hangover, I curse the fool who selfishly drank too much the night before.

The introduction of money into social organization does not just expand our dependence on others through the exchange of current goods, services and ideas; it also permits more complex forms of exchange across time. All financial instruments – from simple debts to complex derivatives – are forms of inter-temporal exchange: an exchange of something now in return for something in the future. Money itself is an inter-temporal contract, because it is a store of value. It does not expire. We assume it will be accepted as a means of payment in the future.

Many informal obligations between people involve time. Parents provide for children when they are young, and children owe them support when they are old. This is a form of inter-temporal exchange. In tribal societies there are many informal obligations to the extended family, which provide for inter-temporal exchange or insurance against misfortune. But money, science and institutional stability have hugely increased the scope and complexity of our relations with the future. Our life expectancy has increased, as has our physical, technological and institutional ability to predict and control the future. But despite the emergence of more concrete and complex futures, our cognitive capacity has not kept pace. An organized temporal future has existed for perhaps a few thousand years, and never to the extent that it exists today. Our brains evolved to be functional in the immediate present. We struggle to be motivated by the future. Often our consideration of our own futures resembles our disposition towards distant strangers. We lack concepts and a language for making coherent sense of the future. This is one of the reasons why we are often confused and inconsistent in our understanding and uses of money and finance.

Myopia and motivation

Cognitive psychologists have a specific term for not caring for your future self: myopia. In finance, myopia is prevalent. *Myopic loss aversion* is a well-researched bias in financial decision-making and thinking; we reveal an excessive concern with short-term changes in the price of investments, often to the detriment of longer-term opportunities. Frequently, we do not reason at all; most people know nothing about their pensions – how they are funded, who will provide them, how secure they are. And often we act quite oddly, continuing to accumulate wealth in old age and as we approach death. These are special cases in finance of a generic tendency to focus on the immediate, often habitually, and give little thought or concern to the future. This myopia does not relate just to active decision-making. It is frequently evident in our preoccupations, beliefs and conversations. Our immediate circumstances often dominate our consciousness. We discuss and are obsessed by recent events, political or economic, which are likely to prove less significant with the passage of time.

Myopia is sometimes rational. We shall see later that not all individuals, or societies, have futures – or at least futures that they can in any way influence or control – so it makes most sense for them to live in the immediate present. But the myopic instinct runs deeper than this. Children have to learn about time. Initially their lives are immediate, and intense. Their empathy is with themselves, right now. That perhaps is true, self-centred, egoism.

Empathy is required not only to understand the interests of others; it is also necessary to care for one's future self. Two distinct aspects of empathy highlight the prevalence of myopia and the difficulty facing reason and motivation, particularly when temporal distance is involved. Some people are very good at empathizing with others in the immediate present. Their empathy is less cognitive and more visceral: they are moved to act immediately to help someone they currently perceive to be suffering. The second form of empathy is more abstract or rational: it is the ability to empathize with those we don't know, whose interests we don't witness directly; it permits us to empathize with those who don't exist, future generations. We might call these two types of empathy "immediate-empathy" and "reflective-empathy", to stress the myopic and cognitive distance they embody. But empathy is not motivation. Empirical studies of moral motivation reveal the role played by discussion, consent, peer pressure and vocal representation of different interests. Abstract and reasoned calculation is not enough to motivate us. Consideration of the future is not just an analytical challenge; it is very hard to be motivated by it. Future generations, and our futures selves, cannot vocally represent their interests. They are destined to have the status of second-class citizens.

Misunderstanding finance

Our brains are designed and have evolved for immediate exist-ence, and their limitations are revealed as our relations to the future grow in complexity. We are not just myopic; we also appear analyt-ically and conceptually constrained. This is revealed in a failure to understand money and finance. Money does not distinguish between now and the future, between us, others, our future selves and future generations. It facilitates trade between these parties for mutual benefit. The most common forms of financial contract that connect us with our future selves are borrowing and saving. We saw in Chapter 1 how banking permits one group in society to receive income on savings and another group to borrow for houses and durable goods they otherwise could not afford. But both saving and borrowing are also relationships with our selves in the future. We save so that in the future we can earn income and spend without working during retirement or if we lose our jobs, and when we borrow we commit our future self to repay.

Many attitudes towards borrowing reflect ignorance about the nature and purpose of inter-temporal exchange. Most striking is the view that saving is good and borrowing is bad. Despite the straightforwardly practical and beneficial functions of borrowing and saving, we have a strange quasi-moral antipathy towards borrowing, and we view saving as virtuous. This view usually reveals analytical confusion: the terms "borrowing" and "saving", in ordinary use, often refer to the same thing, described from the perspectives of different parties to the same exchange. When we talk of savings we usually have in mind saving our money in the bank, or investing our savings in the stock and corporate bond markets through a unit trust or retirement fund. (This everyday meaning of "saving" should not to be confused with the technical term used in economics, which is not relevant here.) But as we have already seen, when you deposit money in a bank, you are lending to that bank. All deposits are loans. Similarly, corporate bonds and shares are liabilities of companies.

A similar failure to understand inter-temporal exchange is evident in some aspects of contemporary Islamic finance, which goes to great lengths to avoid interest payments in a manner consistent with a particular reading of Sharia law. This is futile. Whatever name is used to describe it, interest in some form or another must enter the free exchange of money across time, otherwise it will not occur. Crowds may rage against the exploitative usury of the cruel moneylender, but one seldom hears cries of abuse for the receipt of interest on savings. You cannot have one without the other. Saving and borrowing are different descriptions of the same exchange. Shylock was a moneylender, but in order to lend he must have been a saver. Interest rates are not arbitrary forms of abuse, but payment for risk-taking and for forgoing liquidity and current consumption. It is a plain fact that interest payments are not inherently exploitative. Sometimes real interest rates are negative (when inflation exceeds the rate of interest).

Under such conditions, borrowers are being paid to borrow. This can occur for a number of reasons. It is the "normal" state of affairs in Japan, where the preference to save overwhelms the desire to borrow, primarily for demographic reasons. And as we shall see later, when everyone wants to save it is extremely difficult for an economy to grow.

Similar inconsistencies pervade superficially objective and more technical discussions of international trade. Commentary on the US trade deficit is often presented as though it would be best if all countries ran trade surpluses. Perhaps you are thinking this sounds like a good idea. Unfortunately it is not possible: if one country runs a surplus, by necessity another runs a deficit. This too is an inter-temporal exchange and typically the developed countries that run surpluses have older populations than those with deficits.

So a great deal of our traditional antagonism towards borrowing, while simultaneously praising saving, is based on a lack of understanding. That we are often oblivious to the inter-temporal functions of borrowing and lending is evident in one of the earliest secular critics of usury: Aristotle. His failure to identify inter-temporal exchange is illustrated in the following remark:

> Very much disliked also is the practice of charging interest; and the dislike is fully justified, for the gain arises out of currency itself, not as a product of that for which currency was provided. Currency was intended as a means of exchange, whereas interest represents an increase in the currency itself. (*Politics* I258a38)

But interest is the price of inter-temporal exchange. Interest rates are the price of exchanging funds now for funds in the future. Pensioners would receive no income if borrowers did not pay interest. Aristotle is plainly wrong: borrowing and saving serve essential functions. This fact eludes most thinkers on money through history, not just Aristotle. Even Adam Smith struggles with the idea of borrowing for consumption: "The man who borrows in order to spend will soon be ruined, and he who lends to him will generally have occasion to repent of his folly" ([1776] 1999: 450). This is hardly a ringing endorsement of the credit card from the ideological father of the free market. At least he is aware that interest serves a function, although he views it primarily as compensation for risk and not as a price for inter-temporal exchange (*ibid.*: 200).

Inter-temporal exchange only starts to emerge as a central theme in economic analysis in the mid to late nineteenth century in the works of the Austrian and Stockholm schools, most notably in the work of Eugen von Böhm-Bawerk and Knut Wicksell. Georg Simmel, the nineteenth-century German philosopher and sociologist, in his otherwise exhaustive and occasionally insightful *Philosophy of Money*, published in 1907, barely mentions time. It is not until the work of Irving Fisher in the early 1900s that the English-speaking world started to construct the central problems of economics in terms of the determination of the rate of interest and the inter-temporal substitution of consumption: the exchange of consumption today for consumption tomorrow. It is no accident that this is one of the few areas of economics where genuinely novel ideas have emerged in the past fifty years or so. Under the explicit influence of Fisher's work, Milton Friedman and, separately, Franco Modigliani developed the life cycle hypothesis, which for the first time presents a formal and entirely reasonable case for borrowing to smooth consumption in the face of variable income over one's life-time. This is not just of enormous benefit to the individual, but implies that overall economic activity will be more stable if credit is available to consumers and businesses, a conclusion supported by common sense and some empirical evidence (Dynan *et al.* 2005).

What we owe to each other

Our attitudes are often influenced by how something is described. Robert Shiller explains how we feel entirely different about a financial contract described in terms of "insurance" than one described in terms of "risk" (2003: 83). A savings deposit held with a bank is a good thing, but a loan to a bank is risky. Framing can be wishful thinking if it is merely a pleasing re-description, or it can be enlightenment if it results in deeper understanding. I think of enlightenment as a change in attitude when we understand something better.

My attitudes towards saving, borrowing and finance changed considerably after I studied what was involved, thought about it more and understood their function. I see inter-temporal exchange as one of the main forms of human progress. It allows investment, innovation and insurance. Borrowing by individuals is entirely different from borrowing within the financial sector, which may be aimed at magnifying the pay-offs in a gamble. Personal borrowing serves the economic function of smoothing consumption across time, and allowing us to invest in ourselves, our property or the capital stock. It is entirely sensible for young people to borrow to consume if their future income will be higher than their current income, as is reasonable to expect. It makes sense to borrow for education or to purchase durable goods or houses, using loans that can be repaid through time. Borrowers can use houses and cars today, and pensioners receive income.

Credit cards are much maligned. Most people who use credit cards do not persistently consume in excess of their income. Their credit card gives them far greater freedom in timing their spending, borrowing and saving from one period to another. Credit cards are a form of insurance, providing access to funds in an emergency or for an unexpected opportunity. They are far safer than carrying cash, and often safer than using debit cards. One of the greatest benefits of credit cards is solving the informational problem implicit in all lending. Simmel, writing in 1907, quaintly describes an English businessman, who says, "The common man is one who buys goods by cash payment; a gentleman is one to whom I give credit and who pays me every six months by cheque" ([1907] 2004: 478).

Credit requires trust. Merchants today do not need to be personally acquainted with each individual they serve. MasterCard, Visa or American Express will honour the payment. The exponential growth of e-commerce is helped by credit cards. There is no need to acquire extensive information on the individual making the purchase; and, despite fraud, credit cards provide a greater degree of protection to online consumers than most alternative means of payment.

My perspective on borrowing is also influenced by an awareness of the anthropological origins of borrowing in acts of reciprocity between generations and within families (Lévi-Strauss 1968: 49). It is no coincidence that a major work of contemporary moral philosophy is entitled *What We Owe to Each Other* (Scanlon 2000), because finance has formalized the obligations that existed informally in families. It permits these obligations to hold across large, diverse societies, and between unrelated generations. This is a very different view from the frequent characterization of finance in terms of loan sharks and abusive financial practices: trivial, although no less unacceptable, shares of aggregate financial activity. Would Aristotle have despised lending if he understood insurance and inter-temporal exchange: if he could see the underlying function – that one of money's essential roles is mutually beneficial exchange through time, with our future selves and others?

The former Bishop of Worcester, Peter Selby, provides a contemporary critique of finance in his book *Grace and Mortgage*. Many of Selby's arguments suffer from the inconsistencies I have described. He also emphasizes the costs of finance, without much recognition of the enormous benefits. His book is still fascinating, and I find myself agreeing with many of his sentiments. He is perhaps most insightful when he argues that third world debt imposes huge costs with little benefit. Its function eludes me too. Politicians lending other people's money to other politicians, without the protection of strong institutions, is surely of dubious merit. But I get the feeling reading Selby that he is also struggling to make sense of his own experience. He confesses to having a mortgage. He probably has a credit card, and reassures himself that he pays it off at the end of every month. So he experiences the benefits of credit. But he also witnesses an increasingly materialistic culture, with a desire for instant gratification, and little sense of self-sacrifice for higher purpose. I assume that he had frequent contact through his diocese with people who worried deeply about their debts, and he wonders why they are in this situation. He describes the suffering of poor families burdened by interest payments they cannot meet and threatened with repossession. He may lack an analytical framework to explain coherently these effects, but these are not observations that should be dismissed lightly. To what extent are these generic observations about poverty – or materialism – and not specific problems of indebtedness? Do they point to an intrinsic problem of credit, or can they be mitigated by regulation and support?

It is true that finance is an area where some people will make decisions they subsequently regret. This is hardly surprising if so many learned minds are confused by debt and saving. Dishonest and irresponsible practices will occur, because our ability to calculate and understand risks and legal entitlements is so limited. We will also, without any enticement, copy others in making extremely foolish financial decisions. But these facts are not profound moral truths about the intrinsic corrupting effects of finance. Rather, they provide grounds for the kind of financial innovation advocated by Shiller (2003), such as mortgages indexed to changes in wages and insurance against loss of employment or career risks. And also for regulation. Selby is right that there is a compelling case for consumer information, education and protection, as in many other areas of exchange where consumers' understanding is very limited, such as medicine. But there is nothing intrinsically wrong with borrowing. Its bad reputation is testimony to our ignorance, more so than its costs. Its benefits are silent and rarely articulated, although they are prevalent.

Worry and *Schuld*

I advise skipping this section: you will not like it. I don't feel great writing it; I close my office door firmly, and I will be irritable if I am disturbed. Mention the words "money" and "worry" and we immediately worry about money. I wonder if Bill Gates, one of the richest men in the world, worries about money. I am sure he does, but hopefully not much. If he doesn't, of course, he should. Nobody's money is ever completely safe. Everyone's depends on its recognition and acceptance by others. When it comes to money, worrying seems inescapable. Worry is similar but different from fear. Both can be rational or irrational. But worry is an extended, reoccurring, often minor mental disturbance. We can't always put our finger on what is worrying us. Fear is more physical, usually more intense: the response to a threat. Worries don't have to be threatening; they are subtler, more insidious.

The German philosopher Walter Benjamin is original and thought-provoking, but his greatest attribute is brevity. He often expresses his most interesting ideas in one or two sentences, which is probably why most of his published works are collections of notes. Benjamin does not elucidate his ideas clearly or through well-thought-out logical argument. He makes dramatic, often elusive, statements, and it is up to the reader to find the meaning. A typical Benjamin line can be found in his three-page set of notes called "Capitalism as Religion", the outline of a work he never got round to writing: "Worries: a mental illness characteristic of the age of capitalism" (2004: 290).

Has money, capitalism, created worry? Money serves us by creating a surplus, it facilitates the escape from subsistence. But prosperity is not just a surplus of goods, things, services; it is a surplus of *time*. Worry seems to depend on a surplus of time. This further differentiates it from fear. You need time to worry. People often worry on holidays, or at the end of the day, before sleeping. The surplus of time created by prosperity permits space for worry.

Frequently, we worry about money. It is not difficult to see why. Money, after all, is the means we use to control future risks, and to meet the needs and interests of ourselves and our families. It affects our self-esteem, even though it shouldn't. Is our worry rational, or even reasonable? Often not. By definition, worrying is not functional: it is not reflection, or analysis, or considered decision-making. Worry is a preoccupation that does not resolve itself. Some people respond to worry by "keeping themselves busy"; they are fighting the surplus of prosperity, seeking to eliminate the space it has created for reflection.

Guilt is very similar to worry. It usually describes a preoccupation over how we have treated others. But this is not the full picture. Our concern with the interests of others is equivalent to our relationship with our future self, so too with guilt. We often feel guilty about things that are damaging to our future self. Guilt regulates our behaviour to others *and* our future selves. In Benjamin's notes he alludes to the dual meaning of the German word "*Schuld*": it means "debt", and it means "guilt". This confusion is understandable. Borrowing is an exchange between one's self today and one's future self. But borrowing is not eating chocolate: at least most of the time it isn't. If you still feel guilty, think of it another way: borrowing is an act of generosity from your future, richer self, towards your current, poorer self. Framing may ease your guilt.

I often get asked why "reckless" bankers provided all these crazy loans, repackaged mortgages, securitized loans and subprime loans, most of which were approved during the later stages of the global housing boom, in 2006 and 2007. Was it just naked greed? Greed is a motive for much of human behaviour when money is involved. But I doubt that this is why the senior bankers running most of the world's banks made a series of decisions that proved detrimental to their businesses and to the global economy. After all, they would have made a great deal more money if they had seen the crash coming and positioned themselves accordingly. Bankers are generally greedy; this is obvious – many people are greedy, after all – but that is not what caused their banks to fail. They got it wrong. Otherwise, a great many of them would not have had their own wealth tied up in the same trades, as was the case at Bear Stearns and Lehman Brothers.

Aristotle may not have understood finance, but he had a profound grasp of human behaviour: "Imitation comes naturally to human beings from childhood ... in this they differ from other animals ... in having a strong propensity to imitation and in learning their earliest lessons through imitation" (*Poetics* 1448b5).

We do most of the things we do because others are doing them. That often passes as an acceptable justification. I have little doubt that most bankers running large banks in the past ten years worried a great deal about the complex exposures that their banks had, which they didn't fully understand. But worries can be ignored, pushed to the back of your mind. Typically bankers work very long hours; it helps them not to dwell too much on these worries. But most of all, they took reassurance from the knowledge that everyone else was doing it. This did not mean that they expected to fall from grace in tandem with their peers. No, they assumed it must be okay because everyone else was doing it. In the end, they just ignored their worries. This is why I advised skipping this section. One way to cope with worries is to try to ignore them. Remember, everyone else is doing the same thing, you are not on your own.

Framing and some enlightenment only takes us so far. Worry about money is sometimes warranted. And the more fundamental fact remains: we did not evolve in an environment where we could control, analyse and influence the future. Distant, complex futures, may never sit easily in our minds. Worry is the price we pay for having a future.

Japan and *tokos*

There are also collective worries that are irrational. Shortly after his swearing-in as US Treasury Secretary, Timothy Geithner was quoted as saying in a newspaper interview that the US administration would not "repeat the mistakes of Japan". Japan enters the collective unconscious as a strange economic nightmare. Like many fearful dreams, it is slightly unclear what we are afraid of. If we are honest, we confess to knowing very little about Japan. What do they, the Japanese, think? Is Japan an economic nightmare to the Japanese? When experts talk semi-authoritatively about Japan they usually rehearse the conventional wisdom, which goes unquestioned: Japan lost a decade of growth in the 1990s owing to a financial bubble in the late 1980s and early 1990s, the consequences of which were incompetently dealt with by the Japanese.

One reason why we fail to understand Japan's economic demise, and did not see it coming, is because its origins lie in inter-temporal exchange. It is true that following its boom in asset prices in the 1980s, Japan pursued macroeconomic policy with impressive incompetence. But this has little to do with why Japanese growth declined to a snail's pace in the past fifteen years. The truth is much simpler: the Japanese stopped having children. The direct effect of a declining birth rate on the economy is to lower the future growth rate of the supply of labour. Most of the difference in growth rates across the developed world is due simply to different rates of growth in labour supply. Japan's labour force growth shrank from over 1 per cent in the 1970s and 1980s to an average of close to zero since the mid 1990s. There is good reason to believe that this is the primary cause of the decline in Japanese economic growth, because it is repeated in two other developed economies that experienced equivalent falls in their birth rates, but no financial bubble: Italy and Germany. In Italy's case there is an almost identical decline in growth. Far from being the primary cause of its economic problems, the prolonged weakness of Japan's financial sector is most probably a symptom of the demographic change and its impact on trend growth and equilibrium interest rates.

Earlier generations of economists were much more sensitive to the significance of changes in population growth, perhaps because of the violent and more frequent shifts in the size of the population in the eighteenth and nineteenth centuries. When reflecting in *The General Theory* on the factors influencing the length of a recession, John Maynard Keynes observes: "If, for example, we pass from a period of increasing population into one of declining population, the characteristic phase of the cycle will be lengthened" (1936: 318). The "characteristic phase" that Keynes is referring to is specifically the time that has to elapse after a boom for "use, decay and obsolescence" to cause a scarcity of capital goods and a recovery in investment (*ibid.*). Japan's mix of a boom in investment followed by a sharp decline in population growth is consistent with a prolonged phase of weak economic activity.

A declining birth rate affects the financial sector in a far less obvious way. As I have suggested, interest rates can be thought of as the price that equalizes our desire to borrow with our desire to save. Older, richer people tend to save, and younger, poorer people tend to borrow. Statistically, most borrowing is done by those aged between twenty-five and thirty-five with children, and most saving by those aged forty-five to sixty-five. In a rich society with very few children and many old(ish) people, no one wants to borrow and everyone wants to save. It follows that interest rates are extremely low: there is no return on saving because there is no demand for the funds. Banking becomes an extremely difficult business, because banks make money by transferring funds from savers to borrowers.

Japan's lost decade does genuinely resemble some kind of strange dream. The decline in Japan's growth was partly inevitable because of declining population growth; but actual growth has fallen by more than can be accounted for by a decline in labour supply growth. Conventional monetary policy, which involves lowering interest rates during times of pessimism and raising them during times of optimism, may fail to work if the propensity to save is so high that the "equilibrium" real interest rate is negative. A central bank cannot set its interest rate at a negative number; so what can it do? Print money and give it to households. Why have they never done this? Fear, and a poor understanding of inter-temporal exchange. Japan's "decline" is a failure of thought and will.

Intriguingly, the Greek word *tokos* means both "interest" earned on money *and* "offspring". Perhaps thousands of years ago in ancient Greece someone intuited that finance is an inter-temporal and inter-generational exchange: the number of children we have determines how much interest we earn on our savings.

Is Japan our future?

We are dependent on others today and ourselves in the future. We are also dependent on future generations. The main difference is that our behaviour affects their numbers. Does money or wealth affect the birth rate? Are we all destined to end up like Japan? The evidence is clear that poor countries do have higher birth rates on average, and the transition to higher incomes is correlated with a fall in the birth rate. This may reflect levels of education and access to family planning. But there is more to it than this. In the absence of money, resources and institutions to secure and plan for the future it makes sense to build a clan. Offspring and family serve many of the insurance functions that can be purchased or controlled through savings, and are provided by the state in developed countries (Billari & Galasso 2009). Children can provide labour if the breadwinner suffers ill health; families provide pensions, and care for the elderly. A higher birth rate is functional, as long as parents can afford to keep children healthy.

But why do some rich countries have higher birth rates than others? Japan and Italy have far lower birth rates than Ireland and the United States. It may relate to risk-taking; or perhaps to different social institutions, such as the provision of childcare; or cultural factors may be important, such as attitudes towards women. Is it a form of selfishness or materialism, which is often how the older generations in Italy describe it? If it is, as a strategy it is collectively self-defeating. All the finance in the world can't substitute the fact that someone has to look after us in old age: if not our own children, someone else's.

I find it hard to believe that countries with lower birth rates are more selfish, more altruistic, more rational, more risk averse or less clumsy. Many people have children because their own childhood was positive, or by contrast because they want to prove they are better than their own parents. Some no doubt want children out of self-importance, or for status. All are influenced by their peers. So does money influence birth rates? Maybe. But some things are beyond money's reach. As for Japan, like most bad dreams, we will probably awake and discover that it is not our future at all.

Debt and savings are central preoccupations of our era. Our attitudes towards them are confused and often influenced by prejudices that have persisted for hundreds of years. Money's central purpose is not just to facilitate the division of labour and exchange in the present. Money expands our relationship with the future. Saving, borrowing, bank deposits, shares and bonds: these are all forms of inter-temporal exchange. They are an exchange of income today for income in the future. Inter-temporal exchange has huge benefits: savings and access to credit provide us with insurance, allow us to smooth our consumption over time, and permit freedom over how much, and when, we want to work.

Most value judgements about debt and saving are spurious. Every liability (debt) is also an asset. If some of us want to save, others must borrow. This simple fact explains why all countries cannot run trade surpluses, or why if we all try to save, the returns on our savings – interest rates – will collapse to encourage borrowing. These are facts of accounting and economics. But they still confuse us.

We are not at ease with the complex futures that money, institutional stability and technology have created for us. Worry is one symptom of this discomfort. Sometimes our worries are pragmatic and realistic, during genuine phases of job insecurity or scarcity. But often our worries over debt or savings are confused and unwarranted. Most borrowing by individuals and households is sensible and appropriate. The requisite level of savings for retirement is a trickier calculation, probably indeterminate, and complicated by the fact that retirement is a questionable end-in-itself. (What evidence there is suggests that retirement has negative effects on our health; Dave *et al.* 2007).

Our financial relationship with the future is more complex than the straightforward inter-temporal exchange embodied in borrowing and savings. The future is a source of the unknown, of danger and opportunity. Money is also the means by which we try to protect ourselves, and take risks.

5. Controlling the future

Mystery and denial

The edifice of formal religion has been substantially dismantled owing to a loss of legitimacy, but there is no secular replacement for some of religion's positive functions. There are few structures in secular lives that encourage us to meditate, to reflect on how we treat others, and to discuss these experiences. There is no widely practised secular equivalent of prayer. Those were the positive aspects of the Catholicism I remember from growing up in Ireland in the 1970s and 1980s.

When you grow up in a country where most people share the same religion, you also encounter a very broad spectrum of belief within that faith. The aspects of Catholicism that most appeal to me emphasize how little we know: the virtues of humility, and an acceptance of mystery. When a colleague invited me to attend an Alpha course in the City I was happy to do so. It was organized by the evangelical arm of the Church of England. I have my own personal beliefs about these matters, but am always happy to engage in religious discussion and, almost universally, I have found such exchanges to be respectful and polite, even if prejudicial beliefs are advocated. The meeting took place at lunchtime. We had some sandwiches, and the atmosphere was welcoming and caring, albeit slightly affected. The leader started a factual historical discourse with the explicit intention of showing that Jesus Christ is a proven historical figure: we know for a fact that he existed. (Not many people, myself included, know anything at all about the *historical* basis for Christ, so this was not met with much, if any, dispute.) Once the group accepted that Christ is a documented historical fact, the leader proceeded to make the case for a literal interpretation of the Bible: saying that it is not up to us to interpret or take different views on the Bible, because it means exactly what it says. As I listened to him, I became aware for the first time that his real motive for pursuing a literal interpretation was not just dogmatism or a desire to eliminate dissent. Literalism is also a desire for certainty. If there are multiple interpretations, there is doubt: how do I know that I am following the right interpretation? In the final part of the talk the leader argued that Christianity is the true, and only true, religion. It is right, and everything else is wrong: fact, certain, no doubt.

I looked around the room wondering if I could work out who this talk would appeal to most. I myself was a lost cause, not because of flaws or inconsistencies in the arguments – they tended to be very rigorous – but because I was very familiar with the *strategy* he was deploying. It is a very simple one: eliminate all uncertainty. I have learnt two "truths" from my own work in finance: uncertainty is prevalent, and human beings have a very strong impulse to believe otherwise.

If the future is unknown, why does the past seem obvious?

The human disposition towards uncertainty is influenced by its effect on our self-esteem and our interests. We are more content when we have a clear purpose. We are more comfortable having a defined identity. Hindsight is often a denial of uncertainty, which makes us feel cleverer and better about ourselves. Every day I meet economists and strategists, businessmen, neighbours, friends and family who view developments in the past as certain or obvious which on reflection are not at all obvious. Worse than that, our

Invisible control

Of course, religion does not have to deny uncertainty; it can also embrace it. Recognition of the fragile, uncertain and contingent nature of our lives can also be a source of humility, wisdom and open-mindedness (Vernon 2008: 167). Our attitude towards uncertainty and mystery is ambivalent. Uncertainty engenders fear, but also anticipation and excitement. Beyond our crude attempts to deny uncertainty, what we really want is to control and limit what might occur to our detriment, but pursue what is exciting in our unpredictable future. "You cannot serve both God and Mammon" (Matthew 6:24): in contrast to this widely referenced quotation from the Bible, which sees money as a deity, competing inappropriately with God, I see a very different comparison between money and religion. Money, like religion, addresses our ambivalence towards an uncertain future.

I have argued that although we don't realize it, money has helped create our futures. The most basic functions of money – saving and borrowing – permit exchange between our selves now and in the future. But the future is more treacherous and exciting than this. More things can happen than do happen, and what does happen often surprises us. Unknown futures create scope for invention, surprise and progress, but also instability and danger. Money serves this dual desire to control and experiment. This is the true purpose of financial markets.

Insurance is the financial means by which we seek to mitigate what we fear. Despite its dispiriting and dull connotations, insurance is far more prevalent in our lives than we realize and has little to do with actuaries and insurance companies. Most insurance is implicit and unrecognized. Its widespread benefits are similarly unnoticed. Contractual insurance usually involves paying money now in exchange for money in a contingent future state. It is our attempt to control adverse outcomes that lie outside our direct influence.

The benefits of insurance to the insured are self-evident: it serves to protect us against losses, or our dependents against our death.

Financial markets are markets where people trade *assets*. Money is the primary financial asset; all others could be called derivatives of money. An asset is something that (we hope) has value in the future. Owning financial assets provides insurance. If you save, you protect yourself against loss of work, unanticipated illness or a future change in your working environment that you don't like. Storing cash is a very simple way to obtain this insurance, but not very interesting, and collectively not very useful either. It is also not without risk, because inflation erodes the purchasing power of money and exchange rates can fluctuate, so the purchasing power in other jurisdictions can also change. This, among other reasons, such as inheritance, invention or enterprise, is why people acquire other assets, such as businesses. A business can also provide you with an income in the future.

Now if you own a business, you may be protected (insured) against inflation but you are very vulnerable to anything adverse that happens which is specific to that business. If your family business goes bankrupt, you lose everything. Diversification is insurance against specific risk: if I hold a small proportion of my wealth in a large number of companies I am not significantly exposed to a specific problem at one of these firms. That is why stock markets exist. Their primary function is not to raise finance or allocate capital; they do this very poorly indeed. What they do very effectively is allow owners of businesses to insure against events specific to their business through diversification. Listing on a stock exchange permits widespread, diversified ownership. Bond and credit markets do exactly the same thing for lenders: they are diversified forms of lending. The now infamous mortgage-backed securities sought to do the same thing for mortgage lending.

Although financial markets exist to provide insurance through diversification, most people who work in the world's financial centres are ignorant of the primary function of what they do collectively, and so are regulators, policy-makers, academics and even some finance professors. It is not just borrowing and lending that seem to pose a cognitive challenge. I would guess that maybe fewer than 1000 people in the world, if asked, would say that the principal function of financial markets is to provide insurance. This is a point made with more subtlety by Kenneth Arrow: "Insurance is an item of considerable importance in the economies of advanced nations, yet it is fair to say that economic theorists have had little to say about it" (1984: 78).

Things have progressed a little since Arrow wrote this, but the reflex description of the purpose of financial markets remains the allocation of capital to its most productive uses. This role is in fact primarily fulfilled independently of financial markets, by firms and entrepreneurs themselves, by banks, private equity and venture capitalists. The primary purpose of vast stock markets, bond markets, credit markets, options, futures and other derivatives markets is to provide insurance – protection against contingent losses in the future – through diversification (*ibid.*: 79).

The ability to obtain insurance in varied forms is an end in itself. We want to protect ourselves and our families from theft, illness, loss of income and more modest changes in circumstance. But insurance is also essential to growth in economic activity and prosperity in a world of uncertainty, because it expands our ability to invest, experiment and exchange, all of which are risk-taking enterprises. The Nobel laureate and institutional economist Douglass North describes how "the history of long-distance trade in early modern Europe was the story of sequentially more complex organisation that eventually led to the rise of the Western world". He continues:

[I]nnovations occurred at three cost margins: (1) those that increased the mobility of capital, (2) those that lower information costs, and (3) those that spread risk.

All of these innovations had their origins in earlier times; most of them were borrowed from medieval Italian city states or Islam or Byzantium and elaborated upon in subsequent development. ([1990] 2006: 125)

He is explicit about the role played by insurance:

Marine insurance was one example of actuarial, ascertainable risk; another was business organisation that spread risk through either portfolio diversification or through institutions that permitted a large number of investors to engage in risky activities. (*Ibid.*: 127)

Insurance has a poor image. It sounds dull and tedious, but without it not only would our lives be more treacherous, but we would invest less and take fewer risks. Through diversification, it contributes to the development of trade, to innovation, to risk-taking and experimentation. It is one of the most important ways in which money allows us to control the future. It is a silent contributor to human progress.

Experiments with the future: risk-taking

Insurance reduces the risks inherent in an uncertain future. But our attitude towards uncertainty is not one-sided; nor is it uniformly distributed across individuals. Uncertainty also has a dimension that provides almost universal appeal: it creates excitement, anticipation, the unpredictable beauty of creativity, and risk-taking in its multiple forms. This too is functional. Risk-taking is intrinsic to the most primal human behaviour. It plays a strong evolutionary role. It is present in sexual attraction. There can be no progress without experimentation: as in science, so too in all forms of human behaviour and organization.

Risk-taking, like all experimentation, involves winning and losing, gain and loss. The term "risk" is ambiguous, and its meaning varies with context. But the intuitive concept of risk-*taking* is clearer: it is behaviour involving extreme and usually binary outcomes of gain or loss. The risks involved may or may not be measurable. Many risks we take are not measurable in any way – neither the odds nor the pay-offs – and that adds to their appeal.

There are three broad types of risk-taking: experimentation, investment and gambling. Experimentation and investment are the benign forms of risk-taking. We shall return later to gambling. The time horizon and the nature of the pay-offs characterizes much of the difference between experimentation and investment. Experimentation tends to have more extreme pay-offs: you either win big or lose all. Entrepreneurialism, original research, product innovation or novel organizational practices: these are all forms of experimentation. Often, they either work or they don't. The pay-offs usually include a significant probability of a complete loss of the resources devoted to the experiment. Experimentation is exciting. And even failure produces knowledge: at a minimum the experiment does not need repeating. Investment is central to human development, and often it extends and applies the knowledge gained by experimentation. Investment uses current resources – financial, physical and intellectual – to generate future benefits. Investment involves a calculation or estimation of returns or pay-offs, but the returns accrue over a longer time horizon and they do not have to be binary. The returns to investment can be steady or varied. But there is always risk-taking, because the future is unknown.

Money and financial markets mediate between our attraction towards the excitement created by uncertainty, and our desire for security: between risk-taking and insurance. Markets allow one party to buy insurance and diversify and another to earn a return. Interest is the price of providing funds now in return for funds in the future; the "risk premium" earned by holders of financial assets is the return for the provision of insurance. The distinction within risk-taking between investment and experimentation is mirrored in the institutions of finance. Lending – money now in exchange for money in the future – is one of the main ways we finance more stable, long-term investment, such as infrastructure. Insurance for riskier equity ownership in companies is provided by mutual fund managers, hedge funds, insurance companies and other investors. Venture capitalists are often engaged in financing experimentation: they tend to invest in companies with more binary and extreme pay-offs.

Investors are not attracted to financial markets just by the prospect of earning high returns through financing innovation and growth companies, or the prospect of earning an insurance premium. Some don't realize that that is all they can collectively earn. Many investors are motivated by something similar to a gambling motive, although markets are not zero-sum games. Gamblers would be much better off buying stocks for the same thrill, because in contrast to the casino, where on average you lose, in the stock market you *should* on average make some money (if transaction costs are kept low). Markets are exciting because they are a constant collective attempt to make sense of the future. The insurance premium rises when people are concerned and worried, and falls when things feel safe. People often buy alarms after they have been burgled. More intelligent speculators reason that for similar reasons people will also periodically pay too high a premium for insurance, and they can profit.

Economic progress is in part testimony to the success of financial markets in providing insurance through diversification, and financing innovation and investment. But markets will also be prone to the whims of human emotion. Few of us can behave like detached actuaries objectively assessing risks and seeking diversification. All markets are social activities, and financial markets are no different. They are uniquely interesting because the objective is to guess the path of the future and the behaviour of others. In this way, they also resemble a social, psychological and economic game.

Curing our narrowness of soul

Institutions also provide insurance, and they combat myopia. Trust in others is vital to how we think about the future, and how we care about our future self. It is reasonable to behave *as if* you have no future if you have no trust in the behaviour of others. Institutions formalize the behaviour of others. Weak institutions foster myopia, strong institutions counteract it. Hume sees the origin of institutions in our willingness to be bound by external rules that are in our long-term interest, but that we are unable to adhere to:

> Here then is the origin of civil government and allegiance. Men are not able radically to cure, either in themselves or others, that narrowness of soul which makes them prefer the present to the remote. They cannot change their natures. All they can do is change their situation.   ([1739] 1990: 537)

The German philosopher Jürgen Habermas presents the perspective of the Hegelian tradition in a remarkably similar way: "Hegel's arguments may be understood as asserting that 'abstract morality' demands too high a motivational and cognitive effort from individuals. The deficits must be made good at the institutional level" (2006: 57).

The value of money resides in the responsibility of institutions. They can preserve its value or destroy it. For money to serve its function as a means to control, experiment and invest in the future, we need institutions that we know will behave appropriately and predictably in the future. When monetary institutions lose our trust, as in hyperinflations, this function of money disappears and people seek refuge elsewhere: in the currency of other countries, or in gold, or property – physical assets. Insurance in all its forms, including long-duration securities, life insurance, home insurance and pensions, depends on a stable institutional structure: a reasonably predictable and fair rule of law, government, regulators and, ultimately, social norms. Otherwise it cannot exist. So if you want to know how well a country's institutions function, look at the size of its insurance industry.

Attitude

Long-term investment requires predictability of ownership and rules. Fair and strong institutions reduce required risk premiums and encourage longer investment horizons. But investment also requires something more: a positive disposition towards the future. Attitude matters as much as trust. We know too little about the future for reason alone to be a guide. As Keynes says:

> If we speak frankly, we have to admit that our basis of knowledge for estimating the yield ten years hence of a railway, a copper mine, a textile factory, the goodwill of a patent medicine, an Atlantic liner, a building in the City of London, amounts to little and sometimes nothing.
>
> ([1936] 1947: 149–50)

I was in New York visiting clients on 11 September 2001. My client meeting at the World Trade Center was scheduled for the morning of 12 September, and I was due to meet with an acquaintance at the US central bank, the Federal Reserve Board, in Washington that afternoon. We spoke on the phone and decided to meet up anyway. Trains were still running from New York to Washington. Markets had stayed open in London and so I had some

sense of how people were reacting, which might be useful information for the Fed. We went ahead with our meeting just because it
was comforting to continue. We had coffee and an informal chat. I
spent that weekend in New York and managed to get a flight back
the following Monday. On board, the fear was tangible. To anyone
with a modicum of emotional intelligence this is understandable.
Everyone was shocked. The cabin crew were jumpy and nervous.
One thing was on everyone's mind.

That may have been the safest flight I have ever taken. Or at least,
there was the lowest risk of a terrorist attack. Security has probably
never been tighter or more alert. But it didn't feel safe; everyone was
fearful. Human behaviour in these circumstances is often described
as irrational. We attribute a higher probability to the event reoccurring, than would be deduced objectively.

It is true that some beliefs we hold are irrational, can be shown
to be wrong or inconsistent, but most of the time our attitude to
the future is best described as non-rational. Take the extreme, but
possibly correct, view that we know absolutely nothing about the
future: what would be reasonable to believe or do? Nothing … or
anything. Reason does not dictate a set of beliefs, in the same way
that moral reasoning does not dictate a course of action when there
is an equally weighted conflict of interest. But in the absence of
rational belief, I can form a non-rational one. This is distinct from
an irrational belief, because it does not have to be inconsistent with
known facts.

Optimism is an attitude or disposition that often provides
a non-rational cause for action. It implies a perspective on the
future that is brighter than most. It is not irrational to be optimistic; the future may or may not turn out to be better than most
believe – we don't have the faintest idea. It is non-rational. That is
why there are no genuine entrepreneurs in economics textbooks;
non-rational activity is usually ignored by formal economics. Some
entrepreneurs may be reckless, they make unnecessary errors about

the prospects for their innovation or business. Many, I am sure, are innovators because they enjoy what they do, the creatively unpredictable aspect of their work. But many see a future that is full of opportunity, progress and beneficial change. Invention requires a combination of skill, risk-taking and optimism.

I don't know if optimistic people are happier than others, but they certainly do us all a collective favour. The rewards of innovation and investment occur in the future. It requires money, sound institutions and the right attitude. Optimism, the excitement generated by risk-taking and stable institutions provide reasons to overcome myopia and invest in the future.

The paradox of risk

> If we take eternity to mean not infinite temporal duration but timelessness, then eternal life belongs to those who live in the present.   (Ludwig Wittgenstein, *Tractatus* 6.4311)

I visited Argentina a few years ago, and realized that Argentina is a country where the future does not exist. I realized this because they have no insurance industry. Argentina is a one-period economy; and that period is right now. I am half Italian, and I observed a great many similarities between Italians and Argentines. Argentina is in some ways an extreme version of Italy. Argentines are intelligent, creative and independent-minded, and they don't trust their government or any rules. They rightly view these characteristics as positive. When I say they don't trust any of the rules, this is very different to saying that they don't abide by the rules; it means that they have no reason to believe that rules will be enforced, or enforced fairly. Playing by the rules is a collective action problem. In a country with no rule of law, everyone becomes an anarchist.

Argentines don't have institutions that are consistent through time. Hence no insurance industry. Their form of government has changed: military dictatorship in the 1980s and democracy in the 1990s. But even since the advent of democracy, the rules and institutions of government change frequently and significantly: independent regulators are set up one year, and then lose their independence the next; pensions are "guaranteed" by the state, and then used by the government to fund their borrowing. Little fairness, no stability, no consistency, no trust, no future.

But here is the paradox: if you don't have any future, do you take risks? Of course you do. If there is no future, you have, literally, nothing to lose. You can take risks because you are optimistic, inspired or driven by the prospect of a high return (this is usually functional and benign), or you can live in the present and take risks because you have nothing to lose. Criminality is often an example of the latter. I am not aware of any studies on the risk preferences of different countries. Culture is likely to be only one factor in attitudes to risk; other factors are age and gender. Countries with a strong propensity to risk-taking need very strong law enforcement to harness these attitudes to risk productively, and away from crime. America's success may be in part this combination of a willingness to take risk and a robust legal system.

Argentines take risks, but they don't invest in Argentina. You don't, if you don't have a future. Our relationship to the future is in many ways self-fulfilling: if you don't believe you have a future, you almost guarantee you won't have one. Progress is difficult in a world of instant gratification. But all is not bad in Argentina; far from it. Successful control of the future can be dry and cerebral. Insurance can be dull; Argentina isn't. When you go to Argentina, you have to be careful, but you feel alive.

Time is money

Money does not just expand our relationships with others in a complex division of labour, it also multiplies our relationships with our future selves and others in the future. But our grasp of the inter-temporal is very poor. We did not evolve in a world with an analytically complex and controllable future. So it is no surprise that our understanding of finance is limited. Many of our beliefs about debt and savings are often little better than medieval prejudices.

Religion in part reflects our attempt to find meaning and purpose in an uncertain world; money serves our attempt to control and experiment with an uncertain future. Risks that we choose or take intentionally can be exciting; risks that fall on us to our detriment we seek to mitigate. Money serves both objectives. Insurance sounds dull, but makes life a lot easier and also permits more investment and innovation. Well-developed institutions, optimism and the excitement of risk-taking counteract our inherent myopia. Combined with money and finance, they encourage us to invest and experiment with the future.

There are also costs. Money may have created worry. And people worry a great deal. Understanding may mitigate some of our fears. But the intrinsic difficulties in making sense of the future combined with the allure of risk-taking also make us perfect candidates for mimetic behaviour and occasionally delusional beliefs. We shall return to this: a full understanding requires further knowledge of the properties of money.

6. Other people's money

The securitization of labour

Insurance seems good in principle, as does risk-taking when it is innovation and investment. So where do things go wrong? Insurance involves the assessment of odds and probability. We can get the odds wrong, or we can be unlucky. Sometimes we make collective mistakes: we all get it wrong. Collective error resides in the social nature of markets, a theme we shall return to. We can also be unlucky, extremely bad things can happen that cannot be predicted or reasonably expected, such as certain political events or natural disasters.

There are three other problems with financial insurance and risk-taking: other people's money; leverage with other people's money; and correlation, which relates to luck. These are the oldest problems in finance. Ever since the first stock market was formed, there has not really been any fundamental financial innovation in the nature of money and finance. The same principles, the principles of securitization, have simply been applied to other forms of financial activity. Securitization refers to converting a private contract of ownership into a tradable security. Listing a privately owned company on the stock market is securitization. Shares of ownership can then be traded publicly. Securitization permits insurance through diversification. Money, Marx might have argued, is the securitization of our labour. So there is nothing conceptually novel about the financial crisis of 2008. Only its scale renders it unique.

The securitization of debt markets, which is supposedly the great innovation of the past twenty years, has existed since French bankers started trading agricultural debts in the thirteenth century and was then extended to the first stock exchanges set up in Amsterdam in the fourteenth. Despite its long history, securitization has always posed a problem, which Milton Friedman described more generally, and with reference to government, as "other people's money". It is a particular case of what economists call, less vividly, the "principal-agent problem". Principal-agent problems arise for investors in the stock market because there is an asymmetry of information and a conflict of interest. Managers of stock-market listed companies have far more information about the company than the owners do, so the owners cannot tell if the managers are acting in the owners' interests or performing well. Risk-taking in many large corporations has nothing to do with innovation, and much more to do with seeing what you can get away with without the shareholders complaining or finding out. Often when shareholders complain, they have no power.

The problem of executive remuneration epitomizes this conflict. Today, the ownership of private capital is democratic relative to history: pension funds, insurance companies and individuals saving through unit trusts and other vehicles are the dominant shareholders. They are the principals, and executives are their agents. From the perspective of economic rationality, executive remuneration should meet two criteria. It should align the incentives of managers with the interests of the shareholders they represent: a very difficult task. Secondly, and subject to this first constraint, they should be paid as little as possible. When executive remuneration reaches extremes, this second condition is breached, and company executives resemble an elite trade union.

Luck and correlation

Most principal-agent problems are a nuisance, but not detrimental. People will make huge, catastrophic mistakes with the best of intentions, and in finance they will often do this with their own money as well as others'. Even if principal-agent problems were eliminated, financial crises would still occur. Correlation is a far deeper and more fundamental problem. It is the price we pay for complex interdependence.

Events are "correlated" if they happen simultaneously and share a common cause. Correlated losses are the opposite of diversification. So correlation destroys insurance. When an entrepreneur floats a company on the stock exchange and uses the proceeds to hold a basket of investments, he is diversifying his risk of loss away from events specific to the company he has listed. Car insurance companies write insurance against theft or accidental damage because not all cars crash or are stolen simultaneously. Almost all the time, the loss through theft at the aggregate is far less relative to the income of the car insurance company than it would be to me if my car were stolen and I had to buy a new one. But what would happen if all cars were stolen simultaneously: if car thefts became completely correlated? The insurance company would be bust, and no one would have the insurance they thought they had. The metaphor of putting all one's eggs in one basket is accurate. A correlating event is dropping the basket and breaking all the eggs.

But the principle of diversification is only applicable to particular shocks to the system. So whenever we diversify a specific, particular, risk of loss it becomes apparent that we are still exposed to a more general one. You can put your eggs in more than one basket, but certain events will cause you to drop them all. You can diversify away the risk of an event specific to your family business by selling it and buying a large number of companies, but bigger events can cause all companies to lose value: recessions, nationalization, war, natural disaster. You can try to diversify this risk by taking even smaller holdings in companies across the entire world. And so on. It may well be the case that under certain circumstances everything that exists everywhere is correlated; theoretical physics suggests it probably is. Physics will prove that complete insurance is impossible, if a single event can collapse the universe. For this simple reason, anyone who makes money in financial markets requires some degree of luck. At some level they are writing insurance against an event, which if they are lucky does not occur.

The financial market equivalent to the universe collapsing would be the US government going bankrupt. It so happens that you can buy insurance against precisely this eventuality; in fact I would happily sell you such insurance. It is an intriguing question as to whether it is possible for the US government to default on US dollar denominated debts given that it can print US dollars out of thin air. (Because it can print money, the US government can only default if it chooses to, which it might do if it perceived the costs associated with defaulting to be lower than the costs associated with printing money to pay its debts: inflation and its effects.) But more importantly, the provider of the insurance is unlikely to be in a position to pay up if the US government is in default. If the event or shock is extreme enough, no insurance is worth the paper it is written on.

The individuals who have made the most money in financial markets have usually done one of three things: taken a fee from a large sum of other people's money; taken a hugely risky bet on a given outcome; or provided insurance against an extreme systemic event. In fact, anyone who has a large amount of wealth cannot avoid providing insurance against systemic losses; this is a form of natural justice. How do we reach this conclusion? If complete and perfect insurance is impossible, it is equally impossible to completely avoid risk. The most extreme risk is social collapse, and as we saw in McCarthy's novel *The Road*, when there is social collapse money is useless.

Luck is consequently an ever-present determinant of the distribution of wealth. This is even true of one of the greatest modern investors, Warren Buffett. He is wise, smart and intelligent. Buffett has made his money in two of the three ways we described above: by charging a fee and by providing insurance against an extreme event (the *amount* of money he has made from this is testimony to his other skills). In fact, he provided insurance against the most extreme loss a capitalist can insure: the end of capitalism. Buying stocks in the early 1970s and early 1980s was a bet on the survival of capitalism, particularly as there was then a major conflicting ideology. It is noteworthy that Buffett bought only US stocks. He assumed that the survival of capitalism was most likely in the US. Anyone who buys stocks during a severe economic crisis is really providing insurance against the end of capitalism. That, in part, is why the premium is so high.

Panic correlates

Correlation, or simultaneous loss, can be caused by large shocks that are external to a system. A major change in political ideology or the environment could cause an external shock to the economic and financial system. But any complex system of human organization is also likely to be vulnerable to *correlating behaviour* within the system. Panic is a correlating shock within the financial and economic system. It correlates behaviour because it is self-fulfilling and spreads. It becomes very rational to copy others. If we all fear a recession and save, there will be a recession. If optimism is a public good, panic is the opposite.

It may seem obvious that panic and fear should be avoided at all costs. Yet a fatal psychological error was made by policy-makers in 2007 and 2008 that fostered panic. They discovered new terminology to rationalize their retributive instincts: "moral hazard".

The phrase is misleading because it has little to do with morality. It refers to a conflict of interest that can occur in insurance. You arrive at the airport and cannot recall whether you locked your front door; if you are insured against theft, will you return to check? As a concept in insurance moral hazard is valid and useful in understanding how the presence of insurance can alter incentives and perhaps why some insurance markets don't exist. But it is dangerous when applied to the aggregate propensity to take risk in an economic system. In response to an underlying belief that bankers had gambled aggressively with other people's money in a manner that served their own interests but at considerable risk to stability of the system, central bankers and politicians implied that punishment was due. The chief adherents to this folly were US Treasury Secretary Hank Paulson, President of the European Central Bank Jean-Claude Trichet and Governor of the Bank of England Mervyn King.

"Moral hazard", with its confusing connotations was cited with frequency. We need to teach the deviant few a lesson: fair enough. But by imposing costs on everyone? This is very unwise. A competitive market economy is constantly teaching people about risk, and this is positive when it is specific risk and not aggregate risk. Teaching people lessons by increasing aggregate risk is catastrophic: costs are not borne by specific activities that may or may not reflect inappropriate behaviour; fear is propagated when it needs to be mitigated, panic spreads and is self-fulfilling; everything becomes correlated and many forms of viable risk-taking are destroyed. Panic causes a dramatic increase in risk premiums owing to huge demand for insurance against panic. It creates a surge in demand for cash. Higher insurance premiums require asset prices to fall, so as to offer a higher prospective return.

We do not know whether the extreme nature of the correlated panic that occurred globally in October 2008 was avoidable. It is unlikely to have had a 100 per cent probability of occurring. What is likely is that the doctrine of moral hazard increased the probability of panic. Panic makes everything go wrong at once, like an enormous natural disaster. Recession is the collective price we pay for this perverse "morality".

7. Money measures

MARLOW [gestures menacingly at the big ring on Andre's hand]: That's nice.

ANDRE: What? Oh, you like that? I had it for a long time now, it got some sentimental values. It's just a thing.

MARLOW: What's the real value?

ANDRE: Huh?

MARLOW: Real value. I ain't much for sentiment.

(*The Wire*, Season 4, "Refugees")

Can money measure anything other than itself?

If you can measure, you can compare. If you can measure, you can aggregate. If you can measure and aggregate, you can compute; and if you can compute, technology now permits perhaps limitless sophistication of analysis. But measurement is one-dimensional and always leaves something behind. The cost of measurement is usually measured by some loss of understanding.

Money was designed to value goods and services *in exchange*. Prices are a means to exchange different goods, by a single unit of measurement: money. Exchange in a complex division of labour is greatly facilitated by a common standard of measurement. By introducing a market, money can be used to measure almost anything. In fact, at some point in history, human beings have probably priced everything. Nothing is intrinsically outside the range of exchange.

But price is not value. The term "value" is ambiguous. "Valuable" is sometimes a synonym for "expensive". But often we use the word to describe things we really care about. Monetary value is not determined by usefulness or importance, but by scarcity. Diamond jewellery is hardly useful, although it does twinkle, and can impress, and sometimes more than just impress. Air is essential, but currently free. Clean air may become expensive if it becomes scarcer, as people will attempt to migrate to countries and cities with better air quality.

Marx rightly makes a great deal of the difference between the usefulness of things and the price of things. He uses terminology originally introduced by Adam Smith: *value in use* and *value in exchange*. The terms are self-explanatory: *value in exchange* is price; and *value in use,* refers to the degree of usefulness. Marx identifies the tendency of capitalism and markets to corrupt our sense of the use or true value of things, with an obsession with the monetary value. By rejecting his body of work, economists have ignored this reflexive dimension of price and money. Conventional economics assumes, *a priori*, that we hold beliefs, values and wants independently of the price signals determined in markets. Marx was aware that our attitudes, beliefs and wants themselves change as soon as things are priced, valued or "commodified"; we confuse exchange value with something more, we are seduced by it.

The price of blood

A very striking example of how pricing something might change our attitude towards it was provided in 1970 by a professor at the London School of Economics. Richard Titmuss argued in *The Gift Relationship* that paying for blood donation would reduce the amount donated. Now Titmuss was not just raising a specific point about how best to organize blood donation, he was challenging the neutrality of monetary exchange in social activity.

The significance of this observation was reflected in the responses from two Nobel laureates in economics, Kenneth Arrow and Robert Solow. Arrow's counter-arguments are particularly revealing because he is one of the most original economic thinkers of the past hundred years. But confronted by Titmuss's contention he is surprisingly unimaginative. Arrow's broad argument is the standard economic case for markets. By increasing choice, a system involving payment will induce not just the altruistic but also those motivated by payment to donate blood. So there is no theoretical reason to expect its supply to be reduced. In summary, he says: "Why should it be that the creation of a market in blood would decrease the altruism embodied in giving blood?"

This question reveals the crux of the matter. Even if in the specific case of blood donation Titmuss is empirically incorrect, if he is right that the introduction of a market can undermine our altruistic motivations, this is somewhat unsettling. What surprises me is that Arrow can think of no reasons why the introduction of payment for blood donation might alter the behaviour of those who oppose monetary incentive.

Titmuss identifies an extreme form of reflexivity, from price to character and self-perception, which is very plausible. In Chapter 2, "Money's Morality", we drew parallels between the concept of moral character and reputation in business. Game theory is explicit about the obvious advantages to reputation. Character is similarly important to us. But it cannot be observed directly. Motive reveals character, and character is a heuristic that serves a social function: it allows us to predict the behaviour of others in unknown future circumstances. Our character matters to us. It determines how we are treated by others, and how we perceive ourselves. People of character can be trusted.

We know that people who require blood transfusions are in extreme need. Donating blood is recognition of this extreme need. Receiving payment for this confuses the motivation, implying that we may be giving blood in return for money, and signals a self-serving motive. Money for blood undermines our perception of our character, and probably our beliefs about how others will perceive us. So it is entirely reasonable to object to payment in exchange for blood, and this may influence our willingness to donate.

My best guess would be that the introduction of payment for blood would rarely reduce its supply. Those who already donate blood might find it insulting, but would probably continue regardless. But this does not undermine the generic observation Titmuss makes: measurement in terms of money is not neutral in its meaning or effects. It can alter very significantly our perceptions of ourselves and others.

Measuring worth: how much should nurses be paid?

The ability of pricing and money to change our concerns and self-perception is also central to a minor controversy caused by an economics professor from the University of London. Anthony Heyes (2003) argues that underpayment would attract better nurses. It ensures that they are motivated by vocation, he maintains. Heyes's thesis appears crass and simplistic, but his intention is to provoke thought. In this he succeeds, and his proposal is very revealing.

Forget for the moment the silly notion of "underpaying" nurses, and consider the more general problem of recruiting nurses. It is possible that offering higher wages is not necessarily the best way to recruit more nurses or attract more people to the profession, unless low wages are specifically deterring them. But this does not mean that the reverse is true. It is obvious that nurses, and carers generally, should be decently paid: their work is extremely valuable and it requires a certain type of person to be carried out well. The way to screen for good or bad nurses is probably not through their remuneration, but through their training and subsequent performance.

The important point is that the relationship of remuneration to self-esteem is not straightforward or linear. Ordinarily, nurses are unlikely to be highly motivated by money. But there are a number of very obvious ways to change this. Underpaying nurses in a way that becomes obvious, as Heyes suggests, will undermine their sense of status and implies that their work is not valued. Although not typically motivated by money, they can easily become de-motivated by the implicit signal remuneration sends and by the comparison with others that is likely to follow. Money permits social comparison, and we care about social comparison.

Another way to change their attitudes toward pay is to increase the differentials in pay *between* nurses. This is a signal that does not suggest a measurement of worth relative to other professions, but relative to direct peers. This too is likely to make nurses who are unconcerned about remuneration more concerned. Similarly, offering very large amounts of money to nurses is likely to attract many people who are motivated primarily by remuneration and who are not interested in nursing.

What is true of nursing is probably true of many occupations. It is ideal if people take pride in their work, and this usually requires a perception that their work is valued. The payment of nurses and other carers should take account of this perception. From a purely functional standpoint, this too can be understood as a way of dealing with the informational asymmetries labour economists worry about. It is often impossible, costly and undesirable to monitor and attempt to continuously regulate the quality of someone's work. "Taking pride" in one's work is functionally equivalent to regulation – it is self-regulation – although existentially its opposite.

So how does Heyes reach his conclusions and where does he go wrong? Microeconomics describes human behaviour as an attempt to maximize a set of motivating factors (misleadingly called a "utility function"). Heyes assumes that nurses are motivated by the wages they earn and their vocational calling. As is typical in microeconomics, he further assumes these two "variables" have some degree of "substitutability"; in other words higher or lower wages could compensate for more or less of the "vocational factor". The conclusion that follows from this characterization of their motivation is straightforward: nurses with vocational motives will accept lower wages than those lacking vocational motives (all else remaining the same). There are a number of ways in which this approach is deeply flawed. The main problem is that the ideas we described earlier are extremely difficult to formalize in microeconomics. First, the "motivation function" – it has nothing to do with utility as the term is understood anywhere other than in microeconomics – is far more complex than Heyes's characterization. Our intuitive grasp of human psychology says that it includes the wages of others, and is discontinuous; this means most of the time wages are not a motivational factor at all, because nurses are being paid "fairly", but outside certain bounds, either too high or too low, wages will dominate. Also, many of these factors are not substitutable at all. Indeed, if the government announced that nurses pay was being reviewed on the basis of an interesting paper published by Professor Heyes, I suspect the "vocational factor" would go straight to zero.

Pay-setting in general, and vocational pay in particular, is complex. Nurses are not typically motivated by money, but markets, wages and prices are reflexive and not neutral: they can influence our self-perception, our motivations and our self-esteem. This observation is easily understood after careful reflection. Unfortunately it still eludes much of microeconomics (Becker [1996] is a notable exception). It also defines the limits and costs of markets.

Status seekers

Human beings tend to gravitate towards those they already know: groups with similar educational and cultural backgrounds, often similar professional backgrounds. But we are also socially competitive. Neither money nor markets is the initial source of the introduction to social organization of hierarchy or inequality. Anthropologically, status appears as a functional response to growing numbers and the need to resolve conflict and deploy surplus resources for administration. Larger chiefdoms "tended to have more powerful chiefs, more ranks of chiefly lineages, greater distinctions between chiefs and commoners, more retention of tribute by the chiefs, more layers of bureaucrats, and grander public architecture" (Diamond 1997: 275). Status is functional in societies without formal legal institutions. It serves as a form of constraint, absent an objective and independently enforced legal system. But status has survived as a powerful force despite the redundancy of its original function and our transition to well-ordered societies with objective and universal constraints. We still compete socially, and measure ourselves against our peers.

Incomes are often correlated with status, even in highly egalitarian societies. Vance Packard in *The Status Seekers*, written in 1959, cites an estimate of ten "classes" in Soviet Russia. The income of "managerial specialists" exceeds the mean income by a multiple of five. But even in more extreme forms of social organization where there are no differences in income, there are differences in status. Packard describes the tendency for managerial status to emerge even in determinedly egalitarian organizations, such as Israeli farm collectives, or Kibbutzim.

Money is not the origin of status or its sole determinant, although it is often a dominant cause. Packard describes the struggles of the "old rich" in the 1950s:

> In Northeast City, where I spent several weeks exploring the elite structure of a representative middle-sized metropolis, an old-family social matron talked nostalgically of social relations in the old days. Then, she said, "family" really counted. Many of the best families would never have received the people they do today. But, she sighed, "money is money".   (1961: 34)

Difference in role and purpose is the origin of peace and tranquillity in social interaction. This is often apparent in conversations about children. It is much easier to have conversations about children with people who are younger and don't have offspring. The conversation is free and easy (albeit dull), because there is no implicit comparison. With other parents it is usually trickier. Before remarking on your own children, you must consider carefully on how they will reflect on their own. Money and remuneration permits comparison of status. This is an unintended consequence of money. It is a single homogeneous unit of measurement with no subtle distinctions. In an ideal world, status would reside in character. And money would serve only to price things, and never to value them.

Measuring risk is dangerous

Mimicry is not limited to behaviour; it also dominates human thought. Learning inevitably involves some degree of indoctrination. The educational process requires you to learn the accepted faith before you are in a position to question it. It is a more sensible and safer career path to develop ideas within the conventional framework – after all that is what your superiors have done – than to innovate and render their work redundant. When he reflects on his groundbreaking *General Theory*, Keynes talks a great deal about the need to unlearn what he was taught.

The tendency towards the conventional in education seems to be hardening, which is odd. Measuring ability and the effectiveness of education using examination results is a factor. Education becomes a way of measuring how well you understand received belief. Standardization causes a convergence towards the perceived "standard". But the convergence of beliefs in academia and within the global institutions of economic policy-making is also striking. It may reflect the globalization of beliefs – competing bodies of thought have historically originated in different countries – and it may also reflect the increased structure and professionalization of academia. This is a simplification, but it points to the insights provided by the history of ideas. There was a greater plurality of perspective in the economics and philosophy of the first half of the twentieth century. The body of economics that subsequently emerged left behind many ideas that didn't quite fit or were uncomfortable (White 2005). Many of the ideas that have been viewed as groundbreaking in recent decades are more precise formalizations or restatements of these "forgotten" ideas.

In 1974, a Nobel laureate described a very simple dilemma. If it had been heeded, the 2008 financial crisis may well have been prevented: how do you study complex phenomena if what matters most is not measurable? This question was posed by a deeply conventional and conservative individual, yet it is hard to imagine a proposition more at odds with the spirit of our time. Computation and formal mathematics are immensely powerful tools. If you cannot measure what matters, you are conceding that the deployment of these tools is limited, if not redundant.

The Nobel laureate in question, Friedrich von Hayek, believed that in the study of social behaviour what is most important – the contents of individuals' minds – is immeasurable. This does not render all the statistical work in social science irrelevant, but it defines its limitations, and we should have extreme scepticism when confronted by "empirical evidence". Hayek's Nobel lecture should be required reading for all "risk managers" at financial institutions. The global banking crisis of 2008 can plausibly be described as a failure of risk management. Risk management as it is described in finance textbooks and practised at major financial institutions is a misnomer. To manage risk using the power of computation requires its measurement. But the risks we care about, more often than not, are immeasurable. Formal risk management measures what is available, not what matters.

Words matter

The study of financial risk has been flawed since its inception. Linguistic confusion plays an important part in this story. The origin and history of words, etymology, is distinct from the meaning of words. Confusion of meaning with etymology is a defining characteristic of pedantry. Pedants are not just irritating, but are usually wrong. The meaning of a word does not reside in its history, but in its current usage. That is what "meaning" means. Etymology is rewarding, not because it contains true meaning, but because words can be a store of collective wisdom. Etymology often reveals subtle ideas we have forgotten. Words are often ambiguous, because we use the same words to refer to different concepts, as in the case of "value". Examining the different contexts in which we use words draws our attention to the diverse ideas captured by these ambiguities.

The etymology of "risk" is a story of attempts to confuse our intuitive understanding, which happens to be very apt, with a contrived meaning that is very misleading. Part of the problem resides in a difference in meaning between "risk" and "risk-taking". Risk-taking usually refers to actions involving extreme positive or negative outcomes. It is associated with innovation and excitement. But when, considering an investment, we ask "What is the risk?", we really mean "What can go wrong?" or "How much can we lose?" These two uses of the word "risk" are very different.

I had already worked in the City for ten years before I met someone who accurately described the intuitive meaning of "risk", in the sense of what can go wrong. Dave Fishwick, who I have since had the privilege of working with at M&G, pointed out to me that when we are considering risk in the context of making investments, what we really care about is avoiding *sustained losses*. If you know nothing about finance, this may seem obvious. If you have been trained, you will be forced to think about this. I was. I had been indoctrinated into thinking financial risk was price volatility, which is how it is defined in formal finance theory and at most financial institutions and by most financial regulators.

Volatility measures how much the price of an asset fluctuates over a defined period. If a share price moves up and down by 10 per cent a day it is more volatile than a share that moves by 1 per cent. On the face of it, this seems like a reasonable proxy for risk, in the sense that presumably the share that moves about much more does so for a reason. Sometimes it is true that price volatility genuinely reflects the probability of a sustained loss, but most of the time it does not. Often, price volatility alone has little information, or what information it has relates to things other than risk. Consider the following. A rogue journalist at Reuters, the news agency, sends out a fictitious story announcing a terrorist attack in New York. US stocks fall by 15 per cent. The error is quickly identified by other journalists, Reuters releases a correction and the market returns to its prior level. Volatility of the stock market has just risen dramatically, but it is nonsense to suggest that the risk of owning stocks has changed. Many conventional risk-management tools would dictate that it has; and in order to maintain a stable allocation of risk it would be appropriate to sell stocks!

So why does risk management in finance use the volatility of price to measure risk? One unwitting culprit of this development is Frank Knight, an original and insightful thinker who decided in 1931, quite arbitrarily, to define "risk-taking" as decision-making in circumstances where the probabilities attached to the various outcomes are *measurable*. "Risk", in Knight's terminology, contrasts with his definition of "uncertainty", which is not measurable. Now this definition is idiosyncratic. It is wrong in the sense that it is not the same idea as we intend in our use of the term "risk" in investment – which is sustained loss – or "risk-taking" as we use it in other contexts. Situations where odds or probability distributions are measurable are just that: situations of measurable probability. They sometimes involve risk-taking if the pay-offs are extreme. They have nothing to do with risk-taking if the pay-offs are highly predictable and steady. Knight was aware of this and just used the words in an idiosyncratic way. This is clear from his understanding of competition and entrepreneurialism. In his highly original work *Risk, Uncertainty and Profit*, Knight is really trying to draw a very valid distinction between insurance, which exploits diversification, and enterprise, which earns a return or profit from making investments with highly uncertain pay-offs: risk-taking ([1921] 2006).

Although inaccurate and misleading, the definition of risk-taking as decisions using known, measurable, probability distributions has a great attraction: it permits application of the mathematics of probability. This is why Knight's "definition" of risk survives, although it is wrong. In 1951, contemporary financial theory and risk management was invented, by applying the mathematics of probability to investment portfolios. Modern portfolio theory defines investment risk as volatility; and aggregate volatility is derived from the volatility and covariance of the portfolio constituents. In the classic paper "Portfolio Selection", Harry Markowitz is very explicit: "the investor does (or should) consider the expected return as a desirable thing, and variance of return an undesirable thing. This rule has many sound points, both as a maxim for, and hypothesis about, investment behaviour" (1952: 77).

As with Knight's definition, any subtlety in Markowitz's original ideas is lost in subsequent application by others. His approach *can* be made consistent with the intuitive meaning of risk. Markowitz talks of the volatility of *expected return* and not *price*. He is explicit that historic return distributions are not appropriate proxies for future return distributions. He also assumes, implicitly, that the holding period of the asset is the same as that used to estimate the variance, an assumption ignored by most risk-management tools. In other words, if I am making a ten-year investment, I should care primarily about the probabilities of the range of outcomes over that ten-year period, and not the probabilities of the range of daily returns.* Of course, in reality the issue is much more complicated because our holding period may be contingent or unknown. It is often the case that we make an investment without a clear view of how long we shall hold it. This prior uncertainty over holding periods is not touched on by Markowitz but is addressed neatly by the concept of sustained loss: if we perceive a loss to be temporary, we may choose to extend our holding period. If a loss is permanent, this option has no value.

The view of diversification Markowitz presents is also a striking example of how mathematical insight gets transposed misleadingly into practice. For understandable reasons it is often assumed that portfolios containing a large number of different securities

---

* If you know the mean and the variance of the return distribution, and you assume that the probability distribution is normal, you can define the full distribution. That is the attraction of a normal distribution. Criticism of the assumption of normal distributions in finance is now widespread. Asset price return distributions are rarely normally distributed. This observation is not new. In his *Foundations of Finance*, for example, Eugene Fama notes, "if daily returns are drawn from normal distributions, for any stock a daily return greater than four standard deviations from the mean is expected about once every 50 years. Daily returns this extreme are observed about four times every five years" (1976: 21). Fama also includes a lengthy discussion of Mandelbrot (1963), the first academic to attempt to model more realistic probability distributions.

provide optimal diversification. We described why in Chapter 6, when discussing luck and correlation. Part of the reason we have stock markets is to allow diversification away from the risk associated with an individual company. But what if this risk does not matter very much? What if the risks we really care about affect the whole stock market? Holding the entire universe of stocks is not diversification at all. Now this observation is not inconsistent with Markowitz's theory of diversification. Markowitz shows that it is preferable to create portfolios with multiple assets that do not have *correlated* returns in the desired holding period. Buying a large number of securities, or stocks, is only one, very superficial, way to approach this. Observing actual daily, monthly or historic covariance is suggestive but often irrelevant. What matters is the covariance of their return in *possible future states,* many of which may not be represented in historical data.

The correlation of returns is not written in the past and predetermined; it depends on what happens. If, for example, the stock exchange is suspended for ten years, the return over that ten-year period of a portfolio of 1000 publicly listed stocks will be perfectly correlated, and a portfolio with one publicly listed stock and one privately owned stock will be better diversified. Or consider what may be a more plausible concern: that rising commodity prices act as a constraint on the profitability of non-resource companies in the developed world. A portfolio consisting of the equity of the five lowest-cost producers of resources in the world could provide a negatively correlated positive return relative to a portfolio with a large number of stocks. These examples are entirely consistent with Markowitz's theory, but structuring portfolios to account for these views would find little useful information from historic prices and correlations. Why, then, are historic volatilities and covariances the basis of risk management? They can occasionally be insightful, but for the most relevant scenarios they are not. They are used because they are conveniently *measurable.*

The inherent need for judgement about prospective returns and plausible scenarios cannot be reduced to historic measures of price volatility and covariance. A very similar observation is made in one of the earliest reviews of Markowitz's work, by A. D. Roy, who had developed a similar theory at roughly the same time: "Dr Markowitz presses for a precision in the specification of both motives and of expectations which it seems unlikely that any existing investor can reasonably be expected to possess or to express coherently" (quoted by Bernstein 1992: 63–4). I agree. The main insight from Markowitz (and much of the finance theory that develops subsequently) is simply that covariance matters. And we often forget this: encouraging employees to own shares in the company they work for involves a very high concentration of risk; if the firm goes bust, you lose much of your wealth as well as your income.

The investor Warren Buffett is often presented as opposing diversification. This is an implausible starting-point given that he owns one of the world's largest insurance companies. But he does not pursue portfolio diversification through a large number of stock holdings. As someone with expert knowledge of industry profitability and principal-agent problems, the two main risks he sees are loss of competitive advantage and management misallocating capital. Buying a large number of businesses is a very inefficient way to diversify these two risks if you understand industry economics and can identify good custodians of your capital. Buffett is in fact constructing better diversified portfolios with fewer stocks. Keynes was making a similar point when he said:

> To suppose that safety-first consists in having a small gamble in a large number of different [companies] where I have no information to reach a good judgement, as compared to a substantial stake in a company where one's information is adequate, strikes me as a travesty of investment policy.
>
> (Quoted by Bernstein 1992: 48)

My own perspective is that the value of modern portfolio theory is almost entirely theoretical. I am not suggesting that innovative quantitative approaches cannot be devised to deal with some of these critical subtleties. I expect that they already have by a tiny minority of highly thoughtful individuals. But the mechanical and simplistic application of these ideas that is prevalent in the literature and practice of risk management is detrimental to a true understanding of risk. To draw a contrast with physics: in physics formal theories and empirical estimates are far superior to everyday language at describing many physical phenomena. The opposite is often true in risk management: thoughtful judgement, informed by theory and evidence, is frequently superior to purely quantitative procedures. Subprime mortgage debt and many structured credits had extremely low volatility but were extremely risky, which is why a great many investors avoided them, and many banks using "sophisticated" risk management tools did not. Asian equities had relatively low volatility prior to the Asian crisis, when they were extremely risky, and very high volatility after the Asian crisis, although their risk properties (measured by corporate leverage and governance) were greatly improved. Equity volatility was extremely high in 1999 and 2000, a phase during which a great many equity investors subsequently incurred predictable and near permanent losses, but lower than equity volatility in early 2003, a phase after which equity returns were predictably higher.

Volatility of price is not a measure of the probability of sustained loss. Aggregate risk management at large financial institutions should aim at sustained loss mitigation under conditions of very limited knowledge. Risk managers, which includes any investor, should always be aware of how much might be permanently lost in plausible scenarios. This requires keeping it simple, and being pessimistic when you sense collective optimism. With respect to the latter, the biggest difficulty is finding those who agree with you.

Value is at risk

Money is very good at measuring itself: at measuring prices, costs, revenues and sales. Value in exchange, prices, are intrinsic to the development of markets, and work far more effectively at coordinating complex economic activity than any central planner. The genius of the price mechanism is its ability to aggregate huge amounts of particular and dispersed information – beliefs and wants that are specific to time and place – into a single, simple number for exchange.

But the formation of markets is not appropriate for all human activities, because markets and prices do not just intermediate a given set of preferences, objectives and beliefs. Markets alter us. The effects of measurement and pricing on our behaviour and thought affect everything from the role of markets in vocational professions – such as teaching, medicine, the law and politics – to the setting of executive remuneration, the sensitivity of institutional design and policy approaches to different cultures, and the illusion of quantitative sophistication in risk management. The price of our labour affects our self-esteem and self-perception. Our wealth, whether derived through luck, inheritance or desert, affects our status. Wealth is not a measure of ability, and certainly not of character. As social beings we have a tendency to be hypnotized by prices; this can turn a market that has a basic purpose, such as shelter, into a collective obsession.

Risk is an ambiguous term. Entrepreneurial risk-taking has to do with extreme gains or losses. It is experimental. When we talk about protecting ourselves against risk most of us care about avoiding sustained losses. Some of these risks – those provided by life, health, fire and theft insurance – are quantifiable to a highly useful extent. But the risks that affect our savings and investments are not. The odds cannot be measured, and history is not a quantitative guide. That is part of the reason investing is exciting. The very notion that it can be formalized and measured is questionable. It's risky.

8. The sacred and the profane

Sono conquistatori e noi siamo gl'indiani (They are the conquistadors and we are the Indians). I don't know if this is a colloquial phrase in Italy, or if it was a poetic turn of phrase particular to the Italian taxi driver speeding through the narrow streets of Rome, while chatting freely on his mobile phone. He was referring to the Italian obsession with technology; mobile phones mainly. Italians have been hypnotized and seduced: ironic for natives of the land that invented Gucci, Prada, Ferragamo, Boss and Ferrari.

The conquistadors were motivated by the allure of gold, a shiny, rare, metallic object. The properties of money we have considered so far relate to *functional* properties. Interdependence follows from money's role as a medium of exchange, facilitating the division of labour. The dramatic expansion in our relations with the future follows from money's function as a means to control the future, through insurance, investment and risk-taking. Common standards of measurement are a precondition of mediated exchange, and permit aggregation and analysis. But the importance of these functions does not suffice to explain money's hold over us, and our collective and personal obsessions with money.

Simmel considers money's abstract nature to be its unique property: "money alone ... does not determine its further use" ([1907] 2004: 307). In a barter economy, everything involved in exchange has a specific use. To own something is to use it. But money is abstract, like an idea. Money can be made from any exchange and it can be owned without being used; it can exist without physical presence at all. This abstract property relates to the freedom that money permits. Money can free us from necessity, from employment we do not enjoy, or a society or country we do not like. In the extreme, individuals can be subject to persecution from governments, abusive employers or other groups in society. The invisible, portable and international nature of money offers an individual freedom in a way that no other property right does. In Chapter 2, "Money's Morality", we considered the illusion of independence, which sometimes inflicts the wealthy. But wealth need only be obvious if the owner so chooses. Although property cannot be easily hidden, money can. When the winds change, discretion becomes a virtue. Gold, precious stones and jewellery are also valuable and portable, and have served similar functions in the past.

The various forms of freedom that money make possible can be seen as less obvious forms of the insurance that money provides. But the allure of money runs deeper than this. In Chapter 7, "Money Measures" we observed that monetary value resides not in usefulness but in scarcity. We do not need money to learn this; we are instinctively aware of the value of scarce things. We experience awe when we encounter rarity, even useless or valueless rare things. Perhaps evolution has taught us that something useless today could be useful tomorrow, so a rare object is like a patented technology whose time is yet to come; after all, human beings will even preserve rare bacteria. A rare object has option value. If it is unique, the higher its option value.

Religion has formalized this instinctive attraction to rare and valuable things, and often very creatively developed and used it. Émile Durkheim defined religion using the distinction between the sacred and the profane. Sacred objects or texts are typically rare and often precious. Places of worship are often beautiful. Physical appearance is certainly an aid to the allure of the special or the sacred, but it is not an essential property. Location can distinguish the sacred from the profane; the Latin *pro fano* means "outside the temple". The use of blessings in religious contexts to render the commonplace unique is an inspired device. Holy water is the ultimate transformation of something plentiful and costless into something rare and special.

This is not dissimilar from central banking. US dollars, despite their lack of colour, have an aura of authority. Dollars seem to have more physical presence than other currencies. The design is a combination of simplicity and authority. This is only fully appreciated when you actually hold a dollar bill. Recognition is immediate. In this important regard the euro is a disappointment. Euro notes are thin: they lack charisma. No doubt America's monopoly of the global film industry is a factor in the dollar's role as global currency of choice. Cinema frames many of our unconscious impressions of value and the sacred. A blessing from Hollywood supersedes any other. Only US dollars exist in westerns; surely that is as important to perceptions of value as an independent and authoritative central bank. It is no coincidence that the most enduring image of excess and the corruption of the wealthy during the roaring twenties is that of ostentatious millionaires smoking cigars wrapped in $100 bills. Waste is one thing; burning money is almost sacrilegious.

Pokémania

Whoever created Pokémon cards was a strange genius. He identified the necessary properties of money and created his very own printing press. Pokémon cards are the size of normal playing cards, but with pictures of various fictitious creatures on them. The cards can be used to play a board game, but in practice they are just collected by children. Cards have varying degrees of rarity, and are valued by children accordingly. The makers of Pokémon cards probably did not realize that they were creating not a card game, but a form of private money for children. I became aware of this when my daughter informed me that children exchange food at lunchtime, or toys, for Pokémon cards. They are a medium of exchange, confirming the view that money is one of the "spontaneous" institutions of human organization: Pokémoney evolves independently of any centralized intention.

Pokémon cards are high quality money. They are not just scarce, but also visually alluring. There are shiny cards, with pictures of wondrous beings. If we are honest, we can relate to children's vulnerability to the peculiar allure of valuable pieces of paper. A freshly printed note can have a similar effect: the quiet pleasure of the ATM. Did the designers of Pokémon cards study religious or financial mania when they devised this product aimed at children? Probably not, but they still created many mini-manias across the developed world. The Pokémon mini-mania at my daughter's school has been replicated, I have subsequently learnt, at many schools across the country. As a student of the history of financial speculation, I was familiar with what she described: crowds of children gathered around the entrance to the playground at lunchtime in a frenzy of trading, deception and innovation with the introduction of new cards. Children appealed to their parents to finance the purchase of sought-after cards, occasionally requesting that future pocket money be brought forward, borrowing on margin. Short-selling was not a problem, but there were abusive practices.

"Children started stealing cards, and cheating. Some of the older boys were tricking younger ones out of good cards."

"Mainly boys?"

"Oh yes, they would never have been banned if only the girls had played with them."

I sense a bias. Some psychologists were peddling similar views: that financial mania occurs because men are over-confident (Sibert 2009). No one could argue this with a straight face in the case of the housing bubble: both sexes were equally complicit.

Eventually, the headmaster at my daughter's school took his lead from the crackdown in the City on hedge funds shorting banks, and he banned the trading of all cards. It had the desired effect. Lunchtime games returned to normality, access to the playground was unimpeded and children slept more peacefully at night. A few probably defaulted on the loans from their parents, but that was a small price to pay. (This is the only section of this book where my daughter, spotting the word "Pokémon" out of the corner of her eye, chose voluntarily to read very carefully what I had written. Her father's writing suddenly has value.)

Money's pull on our primitive brain exploits our instinct for property, a desire to protect what is ours, and also our fascination with what is rare and even more so, what is rare and beautiful. One day, perhaps, there will be money with no physical representation whatsoever. Will this alter our attitudes towards it? Criminals will be livid; physical cash is harder to trace than electronic transfer. Banning cash and requiring all transactions to be electronic would be an interesting experiment in crime prevention. Will it cause money to lose its allure? I doubt it. This aspect of money is its most mysterious and illusive property. It is not a rational feeling, it is not obviously functional. Does anyone benefit from the intrinsic allure of money? I don't think so. But a great deal of dissatisfaction, envy and resentment probably follow from it. Envy is a price we pay for our desire to copy others. It is a reflexive response to other people's money: a want that is defined solely in terms of what someone else has. It is particularly malicious because it creates conflict divorced from need.

When people do stupid things for money – behave out of character, lose perspective, become arrogant or aloof – it is worth remembering that aspects of our brains are struggling to cope. Some mental dispositions may serve nothing but destructive impulses. Money's allure can deform us into extreme solipsists. Everything is reduced to one form, one measure: viewed through a single, one-dimensional lens. It is the destruction of the varied multiplicity, the subtlety and complexity of reality and human experience.

It is no coincidence that the most intractable political disputes are over land. Money combines our attraction to what is rare and sacred, with a very deep human attachment to property, a territorial acquisitiveness. Property rights do not appear to be unique to a culture or religion or language. Our sense of ownership of our property and our sense of wrongdoing if it is taken from us are much more essential feelings. I can understand this. Can you ever forgive someone who has taken your property? Even if I wanted to, I would really struggle with this. If someone had taken my property it would eat away at me. Thinking about it increases my heart rate. The only fair resolution is for them to give it back. But what if they believe with equal fervour that it is their's? Worse still, what if the land is believed to be sacred?

9. The other side of the coin

After all, uncertainty and instability are unavoidable concomitants of progress and change. They are one face of a coin of which the other is freedom. (Milton Friedman, *A Programme for Monetary Stability*, [1960] 2001: 99)

Peer pressure

Traders are those who attempt to profit from very short-term, high-frequency changes in asset prices. They are similar to gamblers, in that they are seeking instant gratification, but they are also different: the odds are not stacked against them and are not usually measurable. There can be a very high reward to sophisticated understanding in trading, which is rarely the case in gambling. Are traders in any way useful? If they are it is probably because they provide liquidity, which serves to reduce transaction costs for investors (Black 1987: 152).

Two traders argue about the price of oil. One is a recent recruit to Alpha. He confides this selectively to his peers. He fears that some might question his intellectual competence. He recently read a newspaper article about peak oil: the hypothesis that we are close to the point of maximum global oil extraction. It is a theory that resonates with some of his other apocalyptic views. So he puts forward "his" new opinion that the oil price will rise indefinitely. The colleague he argues with also defies the trader stereotype.

He is not flash and aggressive. He would be thrown by a cocktail menu, let alone a line of coke. He studied economics and mathematics, and is naturally diffident and inarticulate. He recently went on a management course, and he remembers that frequent use of the word "look" makes you sound authoritative. He thinks his colleague is an intellectual lightweight. He expounds the principles of supply and demand: the current level of the oil price will curtail demand, it is self-regulating. He says "look" a few times; and sounds condescending.

Several weeks later the oil price has risen dramatically. The Alpha male sights his colleague in the canteen, and feels immediately uplifted, remembering their argument. Feeling vindicated by this rise in the oil price, and remembering his colleague's dismissal of his peak oil theory, he reflects briefly on how he can raise the subject, without being too obvious. "Did you get a chance to read the peak oil article?", he asks.

Manias, Panics and Crashes, written by the economic historian, Charles Kindleberger, is a wonderful book. Its great attribute is that it does not need to be read. Its title is a perfect, and succinct, description of the history of financial boom and bust. The practical advice that follows from this law of financial history is straightforward: in the midst of a mania, be cautious; in a panic and crash, be brave. The only problem is that manias, and panics, are by definition social phenomena. The arrogant, but rational, trader faces the Alpha male each morning, reminding him that he is "wrong". To go against the crowd can be humiliating. It is against our nature.

The vulnerability of the financial sector to boom, then panic and crash, is an obvious conclusion from economic history, and yet there is little, if any, mention of the financial sector in most economic textbooks. Formal economics has struggled to understand and analyse this central problem, so it ignores it. But this is not true of the three greatest economists of the past hundred years, Keynes, Hayek and Friedman. Far from ignoring recurrent financial instability, they were haunted by it; Friedman and Hayek in particular, because it ran contrary to their fervent advocacy of free markets.

Friedman was perturbed by the process of banks amplifying the growth of deposits through the multiplier, the process we described in Chapter 1, where banks on-lend our deposits, creating new deposits, which in turn are lent, until eventually the total level of deposits in the banking system is a multiple of the original amount of money. Rightly, Friedman views this process as a potential source of instability because banks may have insufficient liquidity to honour deposits. To protect against this requires an extension of government into regulation and deposit insurance. Friedman's monetarism also advocates stable growth in deposits as a condition for stable prices, and he did not like the variability in deposit growth that a free banking system could generate.

Hayek's view of the destabilizing role of the banking system has similarities with Friedman's, but also a significant difference. Like other members of the Austrian school, notably Ludwig von Mises, Hayek was sympathetic to the view that political pressure from the corporate sector on central banks encourages them to hold interest rates "too low". Hayek argued that the Great Depression was caused by interest rates being set too low in the 1920s. This diagnosis resonates today in the popular, and equally uninsightful, view that the 2008 banking crisis was "caused" by interest rates being held too low, specifically in 2003, when interest rates were kept at 1 per cent by the US Federal Reserve Board and at 2 per cent by the European Central Bank. Not only is this a case of hindsight bias, as I described in Chapter 5, but it is also implausible because interest rates will always be low during and after a recession in a world of low inflation. Are we to believe, without empirical or theoretical justification that low inflation necessarily results in repeated financial crises? It is also somewhat suspicious that Hayek blames the Great Depression on policy-makers keeping rates too low during the boom, while Friedman blames their failure to loosen policy during the recession. The only consistency is the desire to point the finger at government.

But Hayek was too insightful a student of financial history to be content with blaming everything on policy error. He sees competition between banks, and the sectoral effects of changes in interest rates, as intrinsically destabilizing. Although incomplete as visions of financial instability, these ideas are pertinent. There is good evidence that financial crises follow periods of deregulation and financial innovation. But this correlation is insufficiently predictive to be of use to an individual bank. A bank executive who is prudent "too early" is unlikely to stay employed. Competition means that it is up to regulators to enforce counter-cyclical lending practices, and they are likely to face political opposition during the good times. So competition between banks plausibly contributes to imprudent lending. Hayek is also right to observe that reliance on interest rates to stimulate the economy will disproportionately affect inter-temporal decisions, or sectors that rely on credit. The boom and then bust of the US auto industry between 2003 and 2009 is a text-book case of what Hayek describes as *relative* price distortion and sectoral misallocation of demand and capital caused by extreme changes in interest rates. This is not just a problem caused by low interest rates. Raising interest rates in response to rising oil prices, a policy pursued by the European Central Bank in 2008, is folly for similar reasons. Higher oil prices are a relative price signal to find substitutes and reduce consumption of oil. Monetary policy should target rising aggregate prices – inflation – which hinders the functioning of markets. It should not be responding to shifts in relative prices, which are the whole purpose of markets. Avoiding sectoral distortions is, I believe, an additional supporting argument for cash distributions to the household sector as an alternative to dramatic reductions in interest rates to support demand. It also points to an unexplored advantage of fiscal policy.

Despite these insights, Hayek does not arrive at the complete theory of business cycles he sought ([1933] 2008: 77). Banks played virtually no role, for example, in the telecommunications, media and technology (TMT) boom and bust, which was a correlated global investment boom financed mostly by wildly overvalued public equity and retained profits. Also, if a sectoral misallocation of capital is occurring owing to collective optimism about prospective returns to a particular area – housing, technology, railways, or emerging markets – raising interest rates may exacerbate this misallocation. As Keynes says in *The General Theory*, raising interest rates may "deter new investment except in those particular directions which were under the influence of speculative excitement" ([1936] 1947: 323).

Friedman accepts a high degree of economic volatility as the inevitable price for progress and uncertainty, focusing his attention on prevention of depressions and the stabilization of inflation. He may be right, but like Hayek he does not identify the role of collective error, let alone mania or extreme pessimism, in amplifying these forces. To do so would grant an important stabilizing role to government, or at least central banks. Friedman veered towards extreme regulation in banking. His policy recommendations for the banking sector are striking because they are so at odds with his strident pursuit of free markets in all other aspects of economics and social organization. He argued the case for draconian restrictions: 100 per cent reserve requirements ([1960] 2001: 69). This requires banks to hold cash reserves with the central bank equal to the value of their customers' deposits. Hayek advocated private money, although I don't think he had Pokémon cards in mind.

It is no coincidence that a theory of asset pricing is absent in the work of Friedman and Hayek, because asset prices reveal a degree of human fallibility, and a tendency towards instability that markets can reinforce. Keynes, by contrast, put asset prices centre stage in his explanation of economic booms and busts. His direct experience as an early hedge fund investor in stock, bond and commodity markets informs his vision. He sees the potential for non-rational hope and fear as ever-present:

> All these pretty, polite techniques, made for a well-panelled board room and a nicely regulated market, are liable to collapse. At all times the vague panic fears and equally vague and unreasoned hopes are not really lulled, and lie but a little way below the surface. (Keynes [1937] 1987: 115)

To Keynes, non-rational thought was an intrinsic part of human life, probably because his first great work was in philosophy and not economics. Like Hayek and Friedman, he saw the advantages of the free market for human creativity, freedom and the use of resources, but he believed that recession and depression were entirely consistent if not inevitable properties of the capitalist system left to its own devices.

One of Keynes's major departures from the economic consensus of his times was his central focus on how we form non-rational beliefs and expectations about the future, the reflexive role the financial sector plays in this process (particularly the stock market), and how this process of belief formation can create economic cycles and, *in extremis*, depressions. This central aspect of his work is largely neglected in what became the Keynesian and new Keynesian schools of economics, because of its philosophical and socio-psychological perspective:

> By "uncertain" knowledge, let me explain, I do not mean merely to distinguish what is known for certain from what is only probable. The game of roulette is not subject, in this sense to uncertainty … The sense in which I am using the term is that in which the prospect of a European war is uncertain, or the price of copper and the rate of interest twenty

years hence, or the obsolescence of a new invention, or the position of private wealth owners in the social system in 1970. We simply do not know.

...

How do we manage in such circumstances to behave in a manner which saves our faces as rational, economic men?

...

Knowing that our own individual judgment is worthless, we endeavour to fall back on the judgment of the rest of the world which is perhaps better informed. That is, we endeavour to conform with the behaviour of the majority or the average. The psychology of a society of individuals each of whom is endeavouring to copy the others leads to what we may strictly term a *conventional* judgment.   ([1937] 1987: 114)

Our propensity to copy and gravitate towards conventional or collective belief is neglected in economics. Game theory, for example, pays only peripheral attention to the notion that some participants are better informed, which implies, as Keynes suggests, that it is reasonable to copy. In many circumstances information arrives unevenly – those closest receive it first – which generates the same result. In the pre-mass media age in which we evolved this was the norm, even if it is not in today's financial markets. Group allegiance, the very basic motivation we discussed in Chapter 3, can also be signalled by expressions of shared belief. These motivations are factors in collective error in the pricing of assets. Markets for assets – financial markets – are driven by beliefs about the future. Our motivations are never straightforwardly rational, and our capacity for reason is severely limited when facing an uncertain future. Confronted by rapidly rising house prices or large changes in stock prices our behaviour is motivated by copying and comparison with others. Collective beliefs prevail over considered and reasonable judgements.

Sad Soros

George Soros is one of the richest men in the world, but he seems dissatisfied. In his internal hierarchy of status, philosophers rank higher than rich people. Soros is clever enough to know that rich people have been lucky. Wealth is rarely a sign of some wondrous ability or talent, although he may view himself as an exception. Great philosophers and thinkers are original and worthy of respect.

Soros is a tragic figure because his theories, which remain ignored by academics, deserve recognition. His central idea has been neglected in part because he is incapable of expressing it in the context of the similar ideas of others. Too much money is perhaps his undoing; it is frequently correlated with vanity. Soros writes on finance as though he has never read the work of anyone else. His main idea is arguably a more general statement of Ben Bernanke and Mark Gertler's financial accelerator, which sees the financial sector amplifying cyclical developments because the availability of credit is affected by the value of collateral, or asset prices, which in turn is affected by the availability of credit.

Soros, like Keynes, gives a more prominent role to beliefs. Keynes suggests that when confronted by uncertain futures we form beliefs collectively and by copying; Soros identifies a separate, explicitly cyclical, component to our beliefs. There is feedback from asset prices to economic reality and back to beliefs. But asset prices affect reality; rising prices improve productivity, foster innovation and risk-taking – so an optimistic premise becomes partially self-fulfilling. Soros assumes that our beliefs about economic reality are biased relative to an objective view of the world. Confirmation from reality then compounds the bias in our beliefs. My colleague at M&G, Dave Fishwick, makes the compelling observation that asset prices themselves have a *direct* feedback on beliefs, a view that complements that of Soros. At any point in time, many individuals are open to a variety of views about the economic outlook or asset prices. Price itself will almost certainty influence which of these views they back, or are inclined to believe. Collective beliefs formed in this way will be self-reinforcing and cyclical.

There is a fundamental tension in any phase of collective optimism, even when it is partly grounded in genuine economic progress, which it often is. As our learning about economic systems develops, and we increase the stability of economic activity and expand the forms and capacity of insurance, we will take on more risk (Samuelson, 2006). Increased stability of the economic system permits scope for increased leverage in financial activity. If economies are volatile, and recessions frequent, leveraged gamblers will not survive. If there is stability, they will propagate. Moreover, our *perceptions* of risk are influenced by a feedback from price. We do not collectively judge the risk of investments by an objective assessment of their true risk properties; we usually view the least risky assets as those that have recently delivered the best returns. Our *experience* of owning an asset influences how we price its risk, rather than an objective assessment of its prospective return. Consequently, the belief that equities deliver the best long-term returns was prevalent in the late 1990s, after the longest equity bull market in history. Japanese investors today believe government bonds are the least risky investment because they are the only asset in Japan to have delivered high returns in the past twenty years, but anyone who invested in the 1970s believes the opposite: that government bonds are the riskiest assets because governments created a devastating inflation in the 1970s.

Hence stability breeds instability. This is probably inevitable, because human beings forget. At some point, beliefs become too optimistic and the process can reverse. If the benign reality depended on optimism and asset prices, their reversal is similarly self-reinforcing. Optimism turns to panic, then fear and recession.

There are deep insights into how cyclical processes unfold in the work of Hayek, Friedman, Keynes and Soros. But none of these perspectives fully grasps the social dimension to asset prices: the peer pressure. After all, a parallel form of all-consuming obsessive behaviour occurs in playgrounds: children will lose sleep and fight over Pokémon cards without banks, uncertainty or biased beliefs. The philosophical properties of money give us a deeper perspective. Soros identifies the effect of asset prices on the beliefs of individuals about the economy; but the impact on self-esteem is just as important. Chapter 7, "Money Measures", describes the reflexive power of money on our self-esteem and behaviour. Even in circumstances where we are not primarily concerned or motivated by money, such as donating blood or the remuneration of vocational workers, our behaviour, attitudes and self-perception can shift qualitatively if money is made important. In asset pricing, this reflexive process is far reaching. House prices – the most social of all asset prices – became a global obsession, analogous to the dotcom boom of the late 1990s. Houses and house prices encroached on conversation and leisure time. The process was amplified by media coverage, and a huge shift in employment towards activities such as mortgage and home selling, and property development (Shiller 2008). Asset prices are not neutral exchange-values, equilibrating supply and demand. They have the power to reflexively hijack social and economic activity.

Competition for status and esteem is intrinsically social: we compare ourselves with others, we don't want to be left out, and we want things if others have them. As Robert Shiller says: "Regret is an emotion ... that provides considerable motivation. Envy of others who may have made more in the stock market than one earned in the past year is a related painful feeling, especially so in that it diminishes one's ego" (2000: 56). The allure of money and asset prices, house prices in particular, play on more than a competitive sense of winning or losing, or status, although all of these are factors. Territorial acquisitiveness is associated with a fight for survival. We learn by copying and mimicking as children, and this instinct never leaves us. Some of this behaviour may be reasonable, but our motives are confused. Social acceptance is associated with being on the same side, even if we have little in common. Although money binds us together, the competitive rush we experience during collective obsessions with asset prices makes us myopic and defensive. There is little care for others, or one's future self. This is not a picture of rational man freely pursuing his well-being, but mimetic man hypnotized by prices, things and money.

Financial leverage

Collective errors of optimism and pessimism combined with their self-fulfilling feedback on reality explain economic cycles. But this is not enough to explain how cyclicality can cause panics and financial crises. The technology bubble was a colossal phase of financial speculation that carried little cost and caused much benefit.

The key difference with the housing recession of 2007/8 is that the TMT bust did not cause banks to fail. Part of the reason banks did not fail is precisely because of the financial innovations of the previous twenty years, and particularly debt securitization. As a result of securitization, loans to the telecoms sector (and Enron) were diversified globally and no bank had a concentrated and debilitating exposure. This observation undermines the emerging conventional wisdom that securitization caused the banking crisis of 2008. The obvious retort to this hypothesis is: why, if the banks had distributed all of the loans through securitization, did they lose any money? If the originator of the mortgage loan knew the risk was so poor, but ignored this fact because they could sell on the risk, why were they left holding these toxic assets themselves? This cannot be explained as a principal-agent problem caused by securitization. Hayek's insight into the effects of competition among banks is probably more relevant. But the primary cause is a collective mistake. Banks held the same exposures on their own books as they had distributed through securitization. When the value of these assets collapsed, so too did their capital. And in almost all cases, the major decision-makers in the banks owned large amounts of equity capital. No clever explanation is required: they got it wrong.

During the TMT boom there was also collective error over the elimination of economic cycles and the prospective profitability of technology shares. Fortunately, the optimism was mainly manifest in wildly volatile share prices. A bank would not survive for a week if it took out highly levered exposure to share prices fluctuating by 5–10 per cent daily, in contrast to house prices, which trend in a much more stable fashion (and price data is monthly and arrives with lags.)

In contrast to the benign forms of borrowing we described in Chapters 4 and 5, major increases in the leverage of the financial sector in response to rising asset prices are usually pernicious. It is analogous to gambling, but with a twist. Gambling is typically a tedious form of risk-taking. It is intellectually uninteresting: the closest thing to predictable risk-taking. That sounds like a contradiction in terms, but the odds in gambling are definable. It is highly predictable that on average you will lose money at a casino. There is little surprise in rolling dice, and no skill. In an attempt to make it interesting the temptation is to raise the stakes, because the underlying activity is dull. Casino gambling is risk-taking for the unimaginative.

One way to raise the stakes is to borrow. Now, I have argued that borrowing is extremely useful when it is an inter-temporal exchange used to facilitate consumption and investment. But borrowing or using leverage to raise the stakes in a gamble serves only to amplify the pay-offs in a game. This is entirely different from borrowing to buy a house to live in or to buy a car or dishwasher; these are functional reasons to borrow that are not directly aimed at risk-taking. If asset prices were predictable, and we all understood their returns and risks clearly, borrowing to buy financial assets would not be problematic. But, as we have seen, most of us struggle to understand the purpose of a consumer loan and the calculation of interest. Understanding asset prices involves far greater complexity and is vulnerable to the correlated and large collective errors we have described (Kurz 2009). Consider the belief held by a great many people in the 1990s: that house prices could not fall (despite the fact that house prices in Japan, Germany and Taiwan, were actually falling for most of the 1990s – if there, why not here?). Our inability to understand asset prices and the existence of principal-agent problems provides a strong case for regulating the amount of leverage financial firms can be permitted. Curtailing *generic* risk-taking throughout the economic system would be detrimental and reduces experimentation and progress, but leveraged gambling is not innovation. In financial markets it is equivalent to writing insurance contracts you have no intention of honouring.

Free money

Asset prices affect economic reality, they affect our individual beliefs about that reality, and they impact social behaviour. Often this process can be extremely benign, such as the technology boom: an explosion of collective optimism and mimetic risk-taking that left in its wake large amounts of investment and a huge amount of innovation. The effects of asset price booms are malign if the financial sector becomes significantly impaired and we fail to address the ensuing recession swiftly and competently.

We understand the process of economic expansion and recession reasonably well. These issues are far less intractable than poverty or economic development. Booms are usually phases of progress. Optimism fosters investment and innovation. It makes sense during these phases to constrain leverage in the banking sector. Leverage amplifies downturns and makes our response more difficult. Hyman Minsky warned us of this, and so did wise observers such as Horace Brock. We ignored these observations; they seemed anachronistic and had not been relevant for several decades. We became victims of our own success. This will always be the case. At some point in the distant future, the lessons of the most recent crisis will also be forgotten.

What is less forgivable is that we also know how to reverse and end recessions, but continue to rely on anachronistic means to do so. Hayek is right, and in all booms there are genuine sectoral misallocations of capital. Many investments made, for example, in property, may never deliver a decent return; just as many dotcom experiments came to nothing. But prolonging a destructive cycle of aggregate pessimism and risk-aversion that destroys productive capacity and our collective willingness to experiment and take risks is a suicidal route to the reallocation of capital. It is correctly described as killing the patient to cure a cold. The market, through relative prices and profits, teaches plenty of lessons during phases of strong growth without us wilfully adding to the risks and propagating fear.

Bernanke (2002) points out that "Keynes ... once semi-seriously proposed, as an anti-deflationary measure, that the government fill bottles with currency and bury them in mine shafts to be dug up by the public". Friedman, more succinctly, recommended helicopter drops of money. Both are suggesting that the remedy for deflationary recessions is costless and simple: print money and let households spend it. There are two ways to do this: either the government can borrow and post a cheque to households, or the central bank can simply credit households with more cash: the purest version of Friedman's helicopter. We have not created the institutional and legal structures to do what Friedman recommended; central banks have printing presses, but they lack helicopters. There is no mechanism for them to print money and give it directly to consumers (Lonergan 2008).

Most industrialized societies have decided that control of the money supply should be given to independent central banks, otherwise money becomes subservient to political interests. But the main features of our central banking institutions have barely evolved since the early parts of the 1900s, and do not have clear legal frameworks or administrative procedures to transfer cash when interest rates reach zero. "Coordinated" fiscal and monetary policy is not a good idea. Fiscal stimulus is not timely, because it is subject to lengthy bureaucratic procedure and implementation, and is easily hijacked by political interests. The simple remedy is for governments to legislate on a rule for cash distributions – an equal distribution across households would be a reasonable starting-point – and for central banks to control the magnitude and timing of these transfers.

In 1933, Keynes wrote:

> If our poverty were due to famine or earthquake or war – if
> we lacked material things and the resources to produce them,
> we could not expect to find the means to prosperity except
> in hard work, abstinence, and invention. In fact, our predica-
> ment is notoriously of another kind. It comes from failures in
> the immaterial devices of the mind.   ([1931] 1989: 335)

Irrational fears associated with remedial policies are still wide-spread: we are nervous printing money, and we feel that recessions are retribution for the reckless. Both these instincts are dangerous. Inflation concerns would be more plausible if we did not live in a deregulated global economy with flexible prices of goods, serv-ices and labour. Prices will rise on a sustained basis only if, after recovery occurs, and optimism returns, we continue printing: a policy no independent central bank would pursue.

Nonetheless, Keynes would be greatly impressed by the response of central banks and governments in 2008 and 2009. Although the means are restrictive and ill defined, central banks have done more within their legally permitted capacities than ever before to mitigate the effects of recession and financial panic. Governments too have been proactive, and policy has been more consistent globally than ever before. If we also emerge with better understood and regulated financial systems, which is possible, the human cost of recession will not have been entirely in vain.

10. Money

Hume describes money as one of the three spontaneous institutions of social organization; the others are language and law. This is testimony to money's usefulness. Its basic functions are enabling and liberating, and expand our capacity to be moral. Money facilitates the division of labour and specialization, preconditions for the productivity that underpins complex institutions of government, and scientific and technological progress. Without it we cannot tame the future through saving and insurance; or innovate, through risk-taking, experimentation and investment. Money finances infrastructure and the arts. Credit makes our daily lives easier and e-commerce viable. We are not just better off; we also have an incentive to counteract tribalism and nationalism. Global money binds us together in a way that profoundly undermines national attachment and interests. This complex division of labour has created global interdependence, and the mutual benefits rely on our differences. If we were all the same there would be little point.

Markets and free exchange are preconditions for these uses of money, and money in turn expands the scope and sophistication of markets. Most analysis of the benefits of markets in the allocation of resources focuses on the effects of incentives: efficiency, improved use of information and innovative risk-taking. These benefits help to explain the continuing global trend towards adopting markets as the principal means of economic organization. The ongoing transformation of living conditions in many developing countries, most notably China, is testimony to the significance of these effects (Wolf 2004).

But the costs of markets and free exchange are not limited to distributional effects, which can be mitigated through taxation. The broader, subtler, costs have been less well defined and understood (Layard 2006). The first step is to recognize that exchange, prices, markets and measurement are not neutral processes that only serve our objectives and reflect our beliefs. The process of exchange and measurement itself influences our beliefs, objectives, wants, character and self-perception. This may help define the limits to the extension of markets into some areas of social organization, such as those where vocational motivations are dominant. But the implications are much broader. It is somewhat ironic that the reflexive effects of markets and money on our beliefs, values and emotions, are starting to be more clearly understood in the study of financial markets. Asset prices do not just serve our needs by equalizing supply and demand. They distort our collective behaviour, influence our collective beliefs and affect our status and sense of well-being.

One way to better understand these reflexive effects is to contrast reality with the stylized ideal presented in microeconomics. Individuals are characterized as having independent, rational beliefs about the world, independent wants and desires. They rationally pursue their objectives in response to price signals. There is truth in this ideal, and it explains many aspects of economic behaviour. But the philosophical properties of money draw out more clearly the unintended effects of money and exchange. Money's capacity to measure is intrinsic to its function as a medium of exchange and unit of account. Measurement does not just provide a price signal that we process objectively in our decision-making. The price of labour affects our status; our wealth affects how we treat others and are treated by them. Volatility of price and historic returns tell us little about true risk. We frequently confuse price and value. We are also seduced by the quantitative tools that measurement permits. In human behaviour, something is invariably lost when we measure. This is true of many things, from examination results to risk-management.

The property of money that seems to cause us the greatest cognitive difficulty is its function as a means to control the future. The prevalence of insurance and its benefits are rarely recognized. Formal insurance contracts are only one aspect of money's insurance properties: credit cards, cash and financial markets all provide forms of insurance against the unanticipated. We are similarly confused by debt and finance, and have been for centuries. Finance and money involve an exchange between now and the future. We struggle to make sense of inter-temporal exchange, and we often deny or are confused by uncertainty. Pick up any newspaper article on the 2008 financial crisis and you will find a failure to recognize that every debt is also an asset, that it is possible to borrow (to buy a house, for example) and save at the same time, and that borrowing more often than not is extremely useful. This is an area where improved understanding alone would be of enormous benefit.

I have argued that interdependence may be the most important property of money, but also that it is ambiguous in its consequences. Money is a social contract: it depends on recognition by others – or it is worthless. The complex division of labour, facilitated by money, replaces violent conflict in social evolution. It transforms those outside our immediate circle of family and friends into people we can cooperate with to our mutual benefit. This is also the origin of a surplus of goods, services and time, which in turn provides for institutions of government and care and protection of others. It is also a process that undermines parochialism and nationalism.

The other side of interdependence is instability and, in the extreme, destructive panic. Fortunately, money itself is the solution, and it costs nothing to make. The greatest difficulties reside in our minds. I recently visited Florida, which has one of the worst affected housing markets in the United States. Five years ago, Florida was in the grip of a housing mania. Today it is experiencing the effects of pessimism, fear and liquidation. There are communities where 70 per cent of properties have been foreclosed; shopping malls where all the shops are discounting their goods, and where many are closing down; car companies are offering price reductions and have too much inventory; more than one in ten members of the labour force are unemployed. But none of this is occurring because people don't want houses, cars or to shop. This has not been caused by a natural disaster. Nor do we need a scientific discovery to remedy this problem.

So why don't we just create money and transfer it to people's bank accounts? Some objections to printing money in these circumstances warrant consideration. Is it unfair? Will it encourage irresponsible or foolish behaviour in the future? This may be a valid criticism of tax breaks or subsidies for homeowners, or incentives to buy cars, as these measures favour specific sectors. But this is not true of an equal cash distribution to all households. There is no preferential treatment or specific relief to borrowers, savers, the unscrupulous or the myopic. A second objection is that giving people cash would be inflationary. This is confused. In a recession the prices of houses, goods, services and cars are falling. Giving people cash will hopefully stop prices from falling and result in busier shops, higher sales and more jobs. At this point it is obvious that you stop printing money and, if the economy starts to recover more rapidly, interest rates and taxes can be raised; this is to be welcomed – it is the objective.

The final concern is associated with the Austrian school. It is an extreme form of free market idealism. This view holds that recession is a necessary process, required for the market to clear. I agree that there can be major misallocations of capital. I have argued that collectively we can make huge mistakes. But the way to solve this problem is very clear: encourage competition, not recession. Recession, by definition, puts out of business many firms that would ordinarily survive and puts out of work for prolonged periods of time many people who should be employed. Deregulated and competitive markets are the effective way to determine which businesses should survive, and where and how people in the private sector should work. There is absolutely no "need" for a slump.

There are institutional hurdles. Economists debate whether these policies constitute fiscal or monetary policy: should they be implemented by central government or an independent central bank? This is easily resolved. The distributional consequences are the remit of elected government, so the rule for the transfer should be decided by government: for example, an equal distribution per household. But the central bank should determine the magnitude and timing of the amount of the transfer. Most countries recognize that setting interest rates should be separated from the electoral cycle and political manipulation. The same is true of control of the money supply.

The real problem is psychological. There is a legacy and irrational fear of inflation. This is spurious, for the reasons I have given, but nonetheless powerful. If you listen to Bernanke testify to Congress on monetary policy or the chief economist of the Bank of England talking at a press conference, neither will openly refer to the fact that they print money as a matter of course. When he was an academic Bernanke argued openly for cash transfers in similar circumstances to those that prevail currently, but he makes no such advocacy in public now. There are less well-defined but equally powerful fears that I have also described. Giving people money is too simple a solution for a grave problem. We have a deep-seated belief that there must be suffering, pain and retribution. There is also an understandable risk aversion towards new policies. Printing money and transferring it to households is unconventional; we don't want to do it because we haven't done it. This is only partially true, however; many countries have adopted policies that are very similar to central bank-financed cash transfers in design and effect. Chinese fiscal transfers have been financed in large part through borrowing from state-owned banks, which is analogous; and the Australian government has made cash transfers to the public, although financed by government borrowing. Unsurprisingly, these economies are showing the most marked recoveries already and have suffered least in the downturn.

We should not be too surprised that such prejudices dominate policy-making. I have argued that our biases, value-judgements and confusion over money's purpose and function run deep.

The final property of money – its allure – is equally revealing of human frailty. It cannot be irrational to be attracted to money; after all, it grants us power, freedom and security. But money also plays on less appealing propensities towards greed, envy and self-importance. The more rapidly our environment changes, the less likely it is that our instincts are functional: the heuristics that supported survival under conditions of extreme scarcity and in futureless environments can be destructive in the contemporary one. We struggle to think independently or make sense of the futures we have created. We have evolved to be myopic, to copy, and to engage in collectively defeating social competition. This often results in a combination of excess and discontent. At extremes, mimetic behaviour combines with the allure of money to create obsession and mania.

I have had a recurring concern in writing this book. There can be little doubt that money would serve us better if we thought about it less. For obvious reasons, I have kept this observation until the end of the book. But if we have an evolutionary trait that stands a chance of being functional in all imaginable environments, it is our capacity for reason and understanding. Beyond the trickery of framing lies enlightenment. Reason permits self-awareness and practical or moral reason creates hope for a universal belief in taking the interests of others into account. Money is very poorly understood. Its functions go unnoticed and are rarely articulated. Our attitudes towards it and its pernicious effects may change if we understand it better.

Further reading

For an account of historical struggles with fiat (paper) money, from an era most of us know little about, Hayek's essays "First Paper Money in 18th Century France" and "The Period of Restrictions, 1797–1821, and the Bullion Debate in England" are well worth reading. They are both in his *The Trend of Economic Thinking* (1991). They also serve as evidence that our struggles with the organization of banking are nothing new.

I found German philosopher Jürgen Habermas's *Moral Consciousness and Communicative Action* (1992) the most successful work of synthesis in moral philosophy I have read. It permanently changed the way I understand morality and made me realize that it is highly likely that moral beliefs, as a matter of empirical fact, are subject to a very clear rational structure. Habermas convincingly outlines the form this structure takes. Habermas is hard work. He is a descriptivist in the sense that he is trying to describe our existing moral intuitions rather than challenge them. He uniquely integrates the work of analytic philosophers such as R. M. Hare and P. F. Strawson with cognitive psychology and John Searle's philosophy of language. He ends up resolving confusions over subjectivism and objectivism in ethics and provides a very plausible and practical description of what we mean when we use the terms "fair", "right" and "moral". The lack of recognition of Habermas's work by analytical philosophers to this day remains surprising. For a stylistic antidote to Habermas, *Natural Justice* by Ken Binmore (2005) draws similar conclusions and is well argued.

Derek Parfit could not be further removed from Habermas in tradition or intent. His main work on identity through time, *Reasons and Persons* (1984), is also difficult. Occasionally he is so relentlessly logical that it feels like an extreme form of pedantry. But it is ultimately rewarding. Parfit does not seek to elucidate and clarify our intuitions as Habermas does: he tries to undermine them.

For a very accessible, but no less profound, take on the proximity of scarcity to immorality, Martin Wolf's *Financial Times* article, "The Dangers of Living in a Zero Sum World Economy" (2007), is well worth reading. If you prefer novels, I recommend *The Road* by Cormac McCarthy. McCarthy implicitly identifies much of what I say about money and morality.

Two books that are encyclopedic in the information they provide on social and economic organization are Jared Diamond's *Guns, Germs and Steel* (1997) and

David Landes's *The Wealth and Poverty of Nations* (1998). Diamond also provides a lucid description of the evolution of society in response to growing numbers, and conflict resolution over scarce resources.

Daniel Kahneman, Paul Slovic and Amos Tversky's *Heuristics and Biases* (1982) is an excellent introduction to the subject. I think the source material is more enlightening than subsequent application of their ideas, for example in finance. Kahneman and Tversky will also irreparably change your attitude towards the medical profession (like the rest of us, they are not very good at interpreting statistics, but their decisions are more important). Nassim Taleb's *Fooled by Randomness* (2004) develops many of their ideas and is a great illustration of the difficulties of being true to how little we know.

As happens with many figures in social science the political connotations associated with Hayek and Marx distort their place in our understanding. Most of Marx's work – his most interesting work, in fact – has nothing to do with communism. When I studied economics at Oxford and the London School of Economics in the 1990s, neither Marx nor Hayek was on our curriculum: Marx because he was deemed to be "wrong", but mainly because his language was unconventional and his subject matter beyond the arbitrary limits that had been imposed on the study of economics; and Hayek because he was deemed too right wing, but also because his ideas too were unconventional and difficult to turn into a mathematically formalized system. Ideas in economics tend not to be measured by their usefulness or accuracy, but by their susceptibility to formal expression, often the step prior to measurement. Marx's enduring insight is not his analysis of specific social and economic relations, because these are not stable and constant and no one can predict how they will evolve. The deeper observation that social relations are determined in part, or at least significantly affected, by economic structure is his enduring contribution. The division of labour has profound effects on our social interactions, which we do not control. Hayek's specific brilliance was to identify how markets aggregate information. He observes that the world is too complex for complete central planning; only individuals have the relevant information to make decisions. If individuals have information specific to time and place, about what they and others want and need, a system that harnesses that information is powerful. Markets use the information particular to each specific time and place and coordinate all this information with voluntary participation. It is difficult to find objective and pertinent introductions to Marx and Hayek. The best is probably Megnad Desai's *Marx's Revenge* (2002). This is also an inspiring book: Desai, a lifelong student of Marxian economics, reinterprets *Das Kapital* late in his career and produces a brilliantly contemporary work.

If you are inclined to pursue the ideas of Walter Benjamin, which I would recommend, read anything by Benjamin, but not cover to cover. Dip in, and reflect at length on his elusive pronouncements.

Finance is a tricky area to get intelligent and direct access. If you are interested in mainstream financial theory, read original source material and steer clear of textbooks, which are dull and usually avoid the relevant stuff. Harry Markowitz's original

paper "Portfolio Selection" (1952) is available at http://cowles.econ.yale.edu/P/cp/
p00b/p0060.pdf (accessed September 2009). It is very clear, and portfolio theory
has not progressed that much since it was written. In fact, the original work high-
lights many of its limitations. Markowitz implies in an interview for the American
Finance Association in 2004, that he recommends using the full history of financial
data – including the Great Depression – to estimate variance. He says: "Somewhere
in the probability distribution there is another 1929". He's no fool. In a similar
vein, I would recommend Eugene Fama's *Foundations of Finance* (1976), available
at http://faculty.chicagobooth.edu/eugene.fama/research/ (accessed September
2009). Again, the original work is far more alert to the limitations of Fama's framework than are subsequent adherents. John Cochrane at the University of Chicago
provides a superb summary of the state of modern finance theory at http://faculty.
chicagobooth.edu/john.cochrane/research/Papers/ (accessed September 2009). He
also makes a case for what has been learnt in the past thirty years. My conclusion?
Not a lot. But judge for yourself. The most insightful analysis of the role of leverage
in finance is by Horace "Woody" Brock of the private economic consultancy, SED.
A sample of his work is available at www.sedinc.com (accessed September 2009).
In contrast to most who call for the regulation of leverage in the banking and
financial system, Woody has a framework for understanding why it is a problem
and why limiting it would be beneficial. Hyman Minsky himself is also very accessible; *Stabilising an Unstable Economy* ([1986] 2008), is a rewarding read. George
Soros has some great ideas, but I don't think he has ever written a clearly argued
book on finance. *Soros on Soros* (1995) is the best exposition of his main idea.
It is also readable because it is a series of interviews. His theory of reflexivity in
asset prices is a more generic version of Ben Bernanke and Mark Gertler's financial accelerator theory. Many of their articles are available on the internet, but they
are very technical descriptions of a simple idea. Bernanke's *Essays on the Great
Depression* (2004) and his speeches are more accessible (available on the Federal
Reserve Board's website; www.federalreserve.gov/ [accessed September 2009]). A
final primer on financial markets would be Robert Shiller's *Irrational Exuberance*
(2000).

If you prefer watching television to reading you probably have not got this far.
But if you have, the HBO series *The Wire* covers many of the themes.

References

Aristotle 1996. *Poetics*. Harmondsworth: Penguin.

Aristotle [1962] 1992. *The Politics*. Harmondsworth: Penguin.

Arrow, K. 1984. *The Economics of Information*. Cambridge, MA: Harvard University Press.

Arrow, K. 1985. *Applied Economics*. Cambridge, MA: Harvard University Press.

Bataille, G. [1967] 1991. *The Accursed Share*. New York: Zone Books.

Becker, G. 1996. *Accounting For Tastes*. Cambridge, MA: Harvard University Press.

Benjamin, W. 2004. *Selected Writings*, vol. 1. Cambridge, MA: Harvard University Press.

Bernanke, B. 2002. "Deflation: Making Sure 'It' Doesn't Happen Here". Speech presented to National Economists Club, 21 November. www.federalreserve.gov/boarddocs/speeches/2002/20021121/default.htm (accessed September 2009).

Bernanke, B. 2004. *Essays on the Great Depression*. Princeton, NJ: Princeton University Press.

Bernanke B. 2000. "Japanese Monetary Policy: A Case of Self-Induced Paralysis?" Presentation at the ASSA meetings, 9 January, Boston, MA.

Bernanke, B. 2009. *Financial Innovation and Consumer Protection*. Speech presented to the Federal Reserve System's Sixth Biennial Community Affairs Research Conference, 17 April, Washington, DC.

Bernstein, P. 1996. *Against the Gods*. New York: Wiley.

Bernstein, P. 1992. *Capital Ideas*. Hoboken, NJ: Wiley.

Billari, F. & V. Galasso 2009. "What Explains Fertility? Evidence from Italian Pension Reforms". Centre for Economic Policy Research (CEPR) discussion paper DP7014.

Binmore, K. 2005. *Natural Justice*. Oxford: Oxford University Press.

Binmore, K. 2009. *Rational Decisions*. Princeton, NJ: Princeton University Press.

Black, F. 1987. *Business Cycles and Equilibrium*. Oxford: Blackwell.

Blanchard, O. & S. Fisher 1993. *Lectures on Macroeconomics*. Cambridge, MA: MIT Press.

Böhm-Bawerk, E. 1890. *Capital and Interest*. http://socserv2.socsci.mcmaster.ca/~econ/ugcm/3ll3/bawerk/ (accessed September 2009).

Bourdieu, P. [1990] 1995. *The Logic of Practice*. Cambridge: Polity.

Borges, J. L. [1962] 2000. *Labyrinths*. Harmondsworth: Penguin.

Brown, A. 2002. "Do You Come From Manchester? A Postcode Analysis of the Location of Manchester United and Manchester City Season Ticket Holders, 2001". Report, Manchester Institute for Popular Culture, Manchester Metropolitan University. www.e-space.mmu.ac.uk/e-space/bitstream/2173/12506/1/season-ticketreport%20-%20brown1.pdf (accessed September 2009).

Cochrane, J. 2001. *Asset Pricing*. Princeton, NJ: Princeton University Press.

Das, T. K. 2009. "A Regret Analysis of Religiosity". *Journal for Interdisciplinary Research on Religion and Science* 4: 215–19.

Dave, D., I. Rashad & J. Spasojevic 2007. "The Effects of Retirement on Physical and Mental Health Outcomes". Andrew Young School of Policy Studies Research Paper Series, No. 07-35.

Desai, M. 2002. *Marx's Revenge*. London: Verso.

Diamond, J. 1997. *Guns, Germs and Steel*. New York: Norton.

Diamond, J. 2005. *Collapse*. Harmondsworth: Penguin.

Durkheim, E. 2008. *Selected Writings*. Cambridge: Cambridge University Press.

Dynan, K., D. Elmendorf & D. Sichel 2005. "Can Financial Innovation Help to Explain the Reduced Volatility of Economic Activity?" FEDs Working Paper No. 2005-54.

Elster, J. 1985. "The Nature and Scope of Rational-choice Explanations". In *Actions and Events: Perspectives on the Philosophy of Donald Davidson*, E. LePore & B. McLaughlin (eds), 60-72. Oxford: Blackwell.

Fama, E. 1963. "Mandelbrot and the Stable Paretian Hypothesis". *Journal of Business* **36**(4): 420–29.

Fama, E. 1976. *Foundations of Finance*. New York: Basic Books.

Ferguson, N. 2005. "Sinking Globalisation". *Foreign Affairs* (March/April).

Fisher, I. [1930] 1977. *The Theory of Interest*. Philadelphia, PA: Porcupine Press.

Foot, P. 2002. *Moral Dilemmas: And Other Topics in Moral Philosophy*. Oxford: Oxford University Press.

Friedman, M. 1957. *A Theory of the Consumption Function*. Princeton, NJ: Princeton University Press.

Friedman, M. [1962] 1984. *Capitalism and Freedom*. Chicago, IL: University of Chicago Press.

Friedman, M. [1960] 2001. *A Programme for Monetary Stability*. New York: Fordham University Press.

Friedman, B. 2005. *The Moral Consequences of Economic Growth*. New York: Vintage.

Gray, J. 2002, *False Dawn: The Delusions of Global Capitalism*. London: Granta.

Habermas, J. 1986. "On Morality, Law Civil Disobedience and Modernity". In *Autonomy and Solidarity: Interviews with Jürgen Habermas*, P. Dews (ed.), 223–7. Cambridge: Polity.

Habermas, J. 1985. *The Philosophical Discourse of Modernity*. Cambridge: Polity.

Habermas, J. 1984. *The Theory of Communicative Action*. Cambridge: Polity.

Habermas, J. 1992. *Moral Consciousness and Communicative Action*, C. Lenhardt & S. Weber Nicholson (trans.). Cambridge, MA: MIT Press.

Habermas, J. 2006. *Time of Transitions.* Cambridge: Polity.

Hayek, F. A. 1937. "Economics and Knowledge". *Economica* 4(13): 33-54.

Hayek, F. A. 1991. *The Trend of Economic Thinking.* Chicago, IL: University of Chicago Press.

Hayek, F. A. [1944] 2004. *The Road to Serfdom.* Oxford: Routledge.

Hayek, F. A. [1933] 2008. "Monetary Theory and the Trade Cycle". In his *Prices and Production and Other Works*, 1–105. Auburn, AL: Ludwig von Mises Institute.

Hauser, M. 2006. *Moral Minds.* London: Abacus.

Heyes, A. 2003. "The Economics of Vocation". Discussion Papers in Economics 03/4, Royal Holloway, University of London.

Hume, D. [1777] 1989. *Enquiries Concerning Human Understanding and Concerning the Principles of Morals.* Oxford: Oxford University Press.

Hume, D. [1739] 1990. *A Treatise of Human Nature.* Oxford: Oxford University Press.

Kahneman, D., P. Slovic & A. Tversky (eds) 1982. *Judgement Under Uncertainty: Heuristics and Biases.* Cambridge: Cambridge University Press.

Keynes, J. M. [1936] 1947. *The General Theory.* London: Macmillan.

Keynes, J. M. [1937] 1987. *The General Theory and After: Part II Defence and Development.* London: Macmillan.

Keynes, J. M. [1931] 1989. *Essays in Persuasion.* London: Macmillan.

Kindleberger, C. [1978] 2005. *Manias, Panics and Crushes.* Basingstoke: Palgrave Macmillan.

Knight, F. A. [1921] 2006. *Risk, Uncertainty and Profit.* Mineola: Dover.

Kolm, S.-C. & J. M. Ythier (eds) 2006. *Handbook of the Economics of Giving, Altruism and Reciprocity.* Oxford: Elsevier.

Kotlikoff, L. 2001. *Essays on Saving, Bequests, Altruism, and Life-cycle Planning.* Cambridge MA: MIT Press.

Krugman, P. 1994. *Peddling Prosperity.* New York: Norton.

Kurz, M. 2009. "Rational Diverse Beliefs and Market Volatility". In *Handbook of Financial Markets: Dynamics and Evolution*, T. Hens & K. Schenk-Hoppe (eds), 439–506. Amsterdam: North-Holland. www.stanford.edu/~mordecai/OnLinePdf/19.Handbook_Chapter_0208.pdf (accessed September 2009).

Landes, D. 2002. *The Wealth and Poverty of Nations.* London: Abacus.

Layard, R. 2006. *Happiness.* Harmondsworth: Penguin.

Lévi-Strauss, C. 1968. *Structural Anthropology.* London: Allen Lane.

Lonergan, E. 2008. "Central Banks Need a Helicopter". *Financial Times* (4 December).

Lowenstein, G. & J. Elster (eds) 1992. *Choice over Time.* New York: Russell Sage Foundation.

Lowenstein, G., D. Read & R. Baumeister (eds) 2003. *Time and Decision.* New York: Russell Sage Foundation.

Malinowski, B. 1932. *Argonauts of the Western Pacific.* London: Routledge.

Mandelbrot, B. 1963. "The Variation of Certain Speculative Prices". *Journal of the Business of the University of Chicago* **36**: 394–419.

Marcuse, H. [1964] 1970. *One Dimensional Man*. London: Sphere.

Markowitz, H. 1952. "Portfolio Selection". *Journal of Finance* **7**(1): 77–91.

Markowitz, H. 2004. Interview, American Finance Association. www.afajof.org/association/historyfinance.asp (accessed September 2009).

Marx, K. [1956] 1986. *Selected Writings*, T. Bottomore & M. Rubel (eds). Harmondsworth: Penguin.

Marx, K. 1961. *Economic and Philosophic Manuscripts of 1844*. Moscow: Foreign Languages Publishing House.

Marx, K. & F. Engels [1872] 1985. *The Communist Manifesto*. Harmondsworth: Penguin.

Mauss, M. [1954] 2008. *The Gift*. Oxford: Routledge.

McCarthy, C. 2006. *The Road*. London: Picador.

Menger, C. 1892. "On the Origins of Money", C. A. Foley (trans.). *Economic Journal* **2**: 239–55.

Minsky, H. [1986] 2008. *Stabilising an Unstable Economy*. New Haven, CT: Yale University Press.

North, D. [1990] 2006. *Institutions, Institutional Change and Economic Performance*. Cambridge: Cambridge University Press.

Nagel, T. 1970. *The Possibility of Altruism*. Princeton, NJ: Princeton University Press.

Ostroy, J. 1973. The Informational Efficiency of Monetary Exchange. *The American Economic Review* **63**(4): 597–610.

Packard, V. [1957] 2007. *The Hidden Persuaders*. Brooklyn, NY: IG Publishing.

Packard, V. [1959] 1961. *The Status Seekers*. New York: Giant Cardinal.

Parfit, D. 1984. *Reasons and Persons*. Oxford: Clarendon Press.

Popper, K. [1957] 1991. *The Poverty of Historicism*. London: Routledge.

Rawls J. [1972] 1991. *A Theory of Justice*. Oxford: Oxford University Press.

Rawls J. 1993. *Political Liberalism*. New York: Columbia University Press.

Roy, A. 1961. "Review of Portfolio Selection: Efficient Diversification of Investments". *Econometrica* **29**(1): 99–100.

Sachs, J. 2005. *The End of Poverty*. Harmondsworth: Penguin.

Samuelson, P. 1958. "An Exact Consumption Loan Model of Interest with or without the Social Contrivance of Money". *Journal of Political Economy* **66**(6): 467–82.

Samuelson, P. 2005. Interview, American Finance Association. www.afajof.org/association/historyfinance.asp (accessed September 2009).

Scanlon, T. 2000. *What We Owe to Each Other*. Cambridge, MA: Harvard University Press.

Selby, P. 1997. *Grace and Mortgage*. London: Darton, Longman & Todd.

Shiller, R. 2000. *Irrational Exuberance*. Princeton, NJ: Princeton University Press.

Shiller, R. 2003. *The New Financial Order*. Princeton, NJ: Princeton University Press.

Shiller, R. 2008. *The Subprime Solution*. Princeton, NJ: Princeton University Press.

Simmel, G. [1907] 2004. *Philosophy of Money*. Oxford: Routledge.

Smith, A. [1776] 1999. *The Wealth of Nations*. Harmondsworth: Penguin.

Smith, J. M. 1982. *Evolution and the Theory of Games*. Cambridge: Cambridge University Press

Singer, P. 1973 "Altruism and Commerce: A Defence of Titmuss Against Arrow". *Philosophy and Public Affairs* 2(3): 312–20.

Sibert, A. 2009. "Why Did the Bankers Behave So Badly?" *Vox* (18 May). www.voxeu.org/index.php?q=node/3572 (accessed September 2009).

Soros, G. 1995. *Soros on Soros*. New York: Wiley.

Stark, R. & W. S. Bainbridge 1987. *A Theory of Religion*. New York: David Lang.

Strawson, P. 1974. *Freedom and Resentment*. Oxford: Routledge.

Sweeney, J. & R. Sweeney 1977. "Monetary Theory and the Great Capitol Hill Baby-Sitting Co-op Crisis". *Journal of Money, Credit, and Banking* 9(1): 86–9.

Suryadinata, L. 2004. *Ethnic Relations and Nation-building in Southeast Asia – the Case of the Ethnic Chinese*. Singapore: Institute of Southeast Asian Studies.

Taleb, N. 2004. *Fooled by Randomness*. Harmondsworth: Penguin.

Tobin, J. 1965. "Money and Economic Growth". *Econometrica* 33(4): 671–84.

Titmus, R. [1970] 1997. *The Gift Relationship: From Human Blood to Social Policy*. New York: New Press.

White, W. 2005. "Is Price Stability Enough?" BIS working paper No 205.

Wittgenstein, L. [1922] 1988. *Tractatus Logico-Philosophicus*. London: Routledge.

Wolf, M. 2007. "The Dangers of Living in a Zero Sum World". *Financial Times* (18 December).

Wolf. M. 2004. *Why Globalisation Works*. New Haven, CT: Yale University Press

Wolf. M. 2009. *Fixing Global Finance*. New Haven, CT: Yale University Press

Vernon, M. 2008. *42: Deep Thought on Life, the Universe and Everything*. Oxford: Oneworld.

Index